Cuckoo Marans in the Taproom

By the same author

SMALL COAL AND SMOKE RINGS

Cuckoo Marans
in the
Taproom

AN INNKEEPER IN THE VALE OF GLAMORGAN

Derek Brock

JOHN MURRAY

To Sylvia, and the children

Text © Derek Brock 1985
Illustrations © John Murray (Publishers) Ltd 1985
First published 1985
by John Murray (Publishers) Ltd
50 Albemarle Street, London W1X 4BD

Typeset by Inforum Ltd, Portsmouth
Printed and bound in Great Britain
by the Bath Press, Avon

British Library Cataloguing in Publication Data
Brock, Derek
Cuckoo marans in the taproom: an innkeeper
in the Vale of Glamorgan.
1. Country life—Wales   2. Wales—Social
life and customs
I. Title
942.9'0858'0924   S522.G7
ISBN 0–7195–4209–X

Contents

Illustrations by Paul Cox

1 · The Bells

QUITE SUDDENLY we had arrived. 'It's a pub,' I said in surprise. 'You didn't tell me you lived in a pub.'

I viewed the building from my little red Morris Tourer with a feeling of apprehension as I held my girlfriend's hand. It was 1954, chivalry still existed, and I was about to meet her parents for the first time. We had courted in the old-fashioned way for four months, yet I had never seen her home, for the simple reason that this was my first day of being a car owner.

The village of Penmark was securely tucked away in the glorious Vale of Glamorgan in splendid isolation. No public transport passed within miles and I later learned that it boasted only two car owners: the publican and the vicar.

'This is the reason I've never introduced you to my father when he's picked me up at Barry each night,' said Syliva. 'He's like a bear with a sore head after a night in there.' She noticed my obvious frown. 'Don't worry, he won't eat you, it's Sunday don't forget, his day off, he's a totally different person on Sundays.'

An English Springer and a Golden Labrador met us at the back door, well-trained dogs who approached us with wagging tails and no jumping.

Mrs Styles greeted me with a friendly but searching interrogation as she continued to prepare the lunch in the flagstoned kitchen. 'I hope you like pheasant,' she said, as I tried to distinguish the two small birds she basted. 'These won't be strong flavoured mind you, we don't hang them as long as the toffs.'

During our conversation, I realised how little Sylvia had told me of her family, and her way of life. Her father came from true gamekeeper stock, hence the pheasants for lunch.

'I often yearn for the good old roast beef and Yorkshire,' she told me, as we strolled down the rear garden to meet her father, 'but we suffer from a mixture of Dad's good shooting and a strong sense of thrift. A couple of cartridges cost a lot less than a joint of beef or lamb, he constantly reminds us.'

We found him stoking a pig-swill boiler in a small shed beyond the large vegetable garden. A tall, strong-featured man with broad, slightly stooped shoulders he gave me a quick glance with a half smile before speaking to Sylvia.

'The blackie's coming over this afternoon, you better muck out the stable, you know how they gossip, don't want them up at the castle to think we're slovenly.' A mischievous glint came to his eyes. 'Even if we are.' He wiped his hand before offering to shake. 'Well, what do you do for a living?'

'A salesman,' I answered with an air of pride in my new-found profession.

'Bloody layabout's job.'

I noticed Sylvia's radiance wilting as I began to flush. 'I don't know about that,' I said, searching my mind helplessly for a suitable answer.

As we walked back to the pub for lunch I felt that my courtship with his only child was going to be turbulent. His appetite was truly enormous, no doubt a legacy from younger days of his legendary strength.

He had many enemies, but all admirers of his beer-keeping prowess and his physical endurance. Part of his earlier days were spent as a drayman's assistant with Hancock's Brewery of Cardiff. They were delivering beer to a Rhondda Valley pub one day when his manhandling of the barrels didn't go unnoticed by a party of miners who had just finished their morning shift. Later, when the two draymen were taking their customary free pints at the bar, one of the miners baited him. 'Bet you can't put a barrel of beer on the counter, mate.' The senior drayman, ever a gambler, immediately began taking bets.

Not too long after I married, I asked my father-in-law if this was fact or fable. His face mellowed into an expression of modesty. 'Aye,' he answered. 'and more the fool for doing it, I had two goes at it. I thought every vein in my body was going to burst, but those miners, they wouldn't let us leave until they had all bought us a pint a man.'

The meal over, he gathered all the left-overs to mix with biscuits for the dogs. He was most certainly a creature of habit, I thought, or was it the sheer routine of pub life. 'You can give me a hand with a couple of casks,' he said to me before going towards the bar.

The cellar was just two steps lower than the bar, indented by the wear of generations of innkeepers who had walked to and fro with pints of ale. Bob Styles had revolutionised the system by drilling holes through the dividing wall and using three-foot-long taps to serve from the bar. There was just one drawback with the system. The eighteen-gallon kils had to be lifted shoulder height up to the stillage. Only a barrel-lifting champion such as he would have evolved such a herculean method.

'Used to sling these up like confetti when I was younger,' he said, sizing me up. 'Old age don't come alone though. Now grab him by the rims and up she goes.'

I wondered why casks changed sex from the floor to the stillage, but I later discovered they were obviously bisexual and illegitimate on off days. After 'horsing up' three casks I was decidedly in favour of the old system, albeit a Christmas card image of a leather-aproned landlord carrying his jugs of ale.

'Why don't you use pumps?' I said in sweet innocence. 'They'd draw the beer up from the floor level surely.'

He answered as he vented the casks with a large wooden mallet and a motor-engine valve – they were lively, sending a spout of beer to the ceiling – 'I could spend the rest of the afternoon telling you why, but in short, beer straight from the barrel is at its peak. A hundred feet away drawn by a beer engine, that's another matter.' He drew two pints from a cask of Home Brew, Hancock's best bitter. 'Here, try that,' he said, 'delivered and tapped two days ago.' Showing a deep amber colour it tasted strong, nutty and fresh. 'Now that cask is at its best. It's stopped working, so I'll change the soft spile for a hard one. It wants to be sold within three days because it's started to deteriorate.'

I began to realise why he had acquired his reputation, as he drove brass taps into the new casks. Later, I helped him carry coal for the bar's fires and with a final dust around it was all ready for Monday morning.

'Only time you can call the place your own on a Sunday,' he said, as we enjoyed another pint and the sleepy fire brought a glow of warmth from the countless array of shining brass and copperware. (But the day was not far distant when most of Wales would be voted 'Wet' on Sundays, and innkeepers, like their English counterparts, would be seven-day-week people.)

'How do you fancy having a go behind the bar?' His abrupt question caught me unaware like so many of his opportune moments during the years to follow.

'Why yes,' was my only prudent answer.

'Make it next Saturday then,' he continued with a triumphant smile, 'that's when we could do with a bit of help.'

The churchbells across the road began their peal. 'Christ,' he said, jumping to his feet, 'I'm supposed to be ringing. I can hear they're a man short, number six is silent.' As he rushed past me towards the ancient arched doorway of the pub I wondered if he ever found time to sleep, but later that evening as we tried to watch the new innovation of television, which had just begun its transmission from Cardiff, he began to snore. I have never heard such a thunderous sound from a human before or since, yet his wife and daughter were immune to it.

He came round at precisely eleven o'clock, as if automated to feed the dogs. My early impression made him appear rather harsh to the animals, who were never allowed in the house, but they were working gun-dogs, trained to a strict discipline. I have since known him to pay a very large sum for a dog only to sell it at half the price because it was not up to his standard. Yet in his way he was extremely kind. Their kennels were very clean and cosy, and their meals were regular to the minute. I recall him spending some time in hospital for rather extensive surgery, and during each of my visits his main concern was the welfare of the dogs and the condition of the beer – in that order. It was midnight before I left after a massive supper of cheese, pickled onions and home-baked bread. The doors were bolted behind me after I made my farewells and I walked eagerly towards my new acquisition, the Morris Tourer. Her battery was lifeless. The last thing I desired, while trying to create the right impression, was to seek their help at the pub.

I began a mental hate campaign against the character who had sold me the infernal machine that very morning. He was a typical post-war used-car salesman, a spiv as they were known by their threequarter-length camel coats over a loud check suit and a snap-brim trilby. 'A little gem you got there, sir,' he constantly repeated as I counted out my hard-saved £110.

I learned later in life that the car was built to sell at £100 in 1936, but this was austerity Britain eighteen years and a world war later!

Fortunately, there is a steep hill nearby and I decided to bump start the Morris in favour of cranking her with the starting handle. The village was utterly lifeless as I pushed and steered towards the incline, only the spasmodic hoot of a barn owl breaking the intense silence of a breathless night. The Morris began to freewheel and I jumped in. Half-way down she started with a savage staccato bark that must have been heard for miles around. The exhaust pipe had rusted away near the engine, giving it complete freedom to awaken the whole village, but worse was to follow: I had to turn at the base of the hill and retrace my route. As I roared to the top like a Le Mans racing driver of the thirties, a light waved across my path. It was the torch of PC Harbottle, the village bobby. The little gem, however, was about the complete her hat trick. As I applied the handbrake, its cable snapped, of all places on the brow of the hill. The situation was ludicrous. I was confronted past midnight by an officer of the Glamorgan Constabulary, a police force well renowned for being paragons of the law. I could not get out of the infernal deafening machine because my foot had to stay on the brake. I dare not stop the engine, for a restart would entail another trip down the hill, but more was to follow as the constable towered above me with a mixed expression of triumph and amazement. The loose-fitting headlamp on the left-hand front wing began to turn with the vibration. Slowly, like a wartime anti-aircraft searchlight it scanned the hedgerow while completing a semicircle to reveal the astonished officer.

'Is there any more?' he said producing his book and wetting his pencil between his lips.

'I'm courting Bob Styles' daughter,' I shouted above the noise. I felt sure those magic words would ensure my reprieve. 'This has all happened tonight,' I continued.

He repeated my words slowly as he entered them into the

book. I recall, the total of charges branded me as public enemy number one, and the fines made a nasty dent into my meagre savings when the case was eventually heard.

All the week I nursed a growing apprehension of my Saturday night début behind the bar.

'The trouble is', said my tutor, after we had consumed one of his wife's enormous teas, 'you have to learn as you go, can't stand here and draw about forty pints, so to speak, just for practice like. Anyhow we'll have one apiece for your first try.'

I held the glass tankard to the tap and half turned the cock. 'No, no, no,' he bellowed, 'that'll be as flat as gnat's piddle, here let's show you.' He held the pot about a foot below the spout and turned the tap full on. 'The cask will always tell you how it wants to be drawn,' he said, as he raised the glass towards the spout to produce a perfect, clear, golden amber pint with a half-inch bubbly white head. He took a generous sip. 'This cask has got a lovely flavour,' he continued, 'but it's a bit on the flat side, so we've got to put the life into it.' He took another draught to half empty the glass. 'Ah, lovely that is, nice and woody, you can't beat the old cheap cooking beer. Now if this cask was lively you'd have to draw him much quieter.'

My hand took on a nervous tremor with my first customer's beer and a liberal amount overfilled the glass to run into the drip pan. I felt his presence to my rear.

'It won't be long before you fill that drip tray,' he whispered. 'That's about eight pints, and I don't filter it back into the cask, so the only ones to thank you are the pigs, who have all the slops.'

I became more skilled as the night wore on and thankfully the level of the drip tray remained a healthy low, but not for the pigs I suspected, who must have been carefree alcoholics by the time their end came about.

Later, as we sat around the fire with the rest of the Saturday casual bar staff, a cheery fellow with a high-pitched voice and the nickname of 'Squeaker', Bob Styles continued on his pet subject of beer management. 'Do you know,' he said as we supped our well-earned drinks, 'one of the brewers once told me, when I was a drayman, that beer is more prone to bacteria than milk, yet you don't see them pulling pints of that all over their hands in a smoky atmosphere then return it to the container to sell again.'

'Squeaker', a fellow bell ringer, with a demanding thirst, supported him. 'Aye, beer's a funny thing to keep. No one ever tells you your whisky's off or your sherry's flat, and that makes treble the profit with no problems in looking after it.'

I happened to notice Bob Styles as 'Squeaker' spoke; he was most definitely assessing me, but for what? His future son-in-law, his successor to the inn, or both, for as the months progressed I became the regular Saturday evening barman at the Bells, as most people referred to it. He began to spend more time on the other side of the counter, and while he remained the figurehead, many of his landlord's duties seemed to be deviously passed on to me, such as the apparent high honour of calling 'Time'. I soon realised why he had quickly relinquished this ominous duty when my hard-earned popularity began to wane, for the public in general, I discovered, have a natural resistance to pub 'Time' callers, they go completely deaf. Over the years that followed I shouted loud, I cooed softly and politely, I rang the bell until the clapper broke, I called at each table to seek their co-operation as I emptied the ash tray while awaiting their elusive glasses, that contained the last deficient mouthful. I was no longer the nice young man who had served them all evening, I had grown horns, and I represented all that was evil to the cause of liberty, democracy and civil rights. They little realised that I would dearly have wished to sell them more drinks, were it not for the paranoiac fear of the sudden appearance of the law.

'You're far too sharp on the clock,' said the spokesman at one particularly slow table. 'We didn't leave the Dragon until nearly midnight last week.'

I was lost for an answer until my father-in-law came to my rescue. 'Aye, and look how you're spouting off about it for everyone to hear,' he said with slight flare of temper.

'Getting 'em out is the hardest part of the trade, I reckon,' he said later as we sat down to enjoy our well-earned pints, in the silent smoke-laden bar. 'You ask any of them to work overtime for nothing, because that's what it amounts to, in fact it's a loss situation when all the overheads remain, and no money is going into the till.' He quoted one character landlord nearby who nightly shouted to stubborn after-time drinkers: 'I've had your money, now bugger off if you please.' The strange thing was the success of his unorthodox mannerism, to which no one took offence, and I know of another very successful inn situated deeper into the Vale of Glamorgan where the licensee was blatantly rude to his customers, but his trade flourished. Perhaps that is the reason that my father-in-law's personal licensee's sign is still proudly displayed in hommage at the bar of the Bells by his successors, for he had a notorious reputation to his abrupt character.

To him the bar and its customers were secondary to the cellar, a shrine whence the elixir of life was created, and God help the poor mortal who dared to complain, after his endless efforts to purvey the perfect beer for which he was so well renowned. He was a publican when good beer-keeping was an art soon to be lost with the advent of fancy-named expensive keg beers, and their CO_2 gas cylinders. He worked in the days when Best Worthington had to be dry-hopped in the cellar and when delicate high-gravity ales such as Hancock's Home Brew pale ale could be ruined by the atmospheric pressure change of a thunderstorm. There was no fancy air-conditioning for the ancient Six Bells cellar; he controlled the temperature fluctuations with wet sacks and hosepipes in the summer, and a variety of all available electric fires in the winter, but the beer rarely moved from its perfection of 54°F.

Even the bottled ales of those days were sensitive to adverse conditions and beers such as the excellent Worthington White Shield had to be poured with extreme care and skill to trap the heavy sediment in the shoulder of the bottle. This particular drink had devout consumers who appeared to enjoy its meticulous preparation equally as much as its exquisite flavour, but alas it was scorned by most busy bar staff who succeeded only in serving it at speed as a glass of unrecognisable murky liquid. One irate learner barmaid complained bitterly to father-in-law after serving a bottle of Worthington with a disastrous result. 'That's the fourth one,' she said, repairing her elegant fingernails with an ever-ready sandpaper stick. 'They've all gone off.' When he showed her how to pour one correctly she stormed away to serve another customer saying 'There should be serving instructions on the label with such a fussy beer.' I suppose she was right, but vintage ports have no instructions and they sometimes have to be poured with the same care as nitroglycerine or sediment will enter the glass.

But I later discovered that bar staff were as unpredictable as the sensitive beer they served. A very small percentage were proud of their skills while the majority carried out the demanding and extremely tiring work purely as a wage-earning job. Their physical aspect was also a debatable subject, for when my father-in-law introduced a big-breasted barmaid as a crowd puller, she did just that, to attract a fine influx of enchanted males who succeeded in completely blockading the counter from all other customers. It also gave the pub an imbalance and he received glares of dissension from abandoned wives and girlfriends who were not so well endowed, when their men spent an unduly long time at the bar. He finally compromised with an attractive matron in her early forties who relieved the pub of its lustful atmosphere to satisfy the tastes of most, if not all, his customers.

His devious training methods for me continued when he commandeered my services during a short holiday period.

'I want you to go into the brewery,' he said, ignoring my frown to Sylvia, who had arranged to take a drive with me in the refurbished Morris. 'Take my car and the trailer for a load of spent hops for the pigs will you?' He had a cunning way of turning an order into a request that was always difficult to resist.

'Do you want to come?' I asked Sylvia submissively.

She stormed off to her bedroom, leaving a protest trail of her coat, handbag, scarf and shoes as she answered me. 'No, I can't stand the smell of the place. He's taken me there all my life to get his smelly old hops, and I'm not going anymore.'

He looked at me guiltily as her voice ceased with a loud slam of her door. 'I'd go myself, but the wife's gone out for the day with the church women's guild, and the pigs are crying out for hops, haven't had any for a week or so, still you'd better take her out or you'll never hear the end of it; pity, too, I got a brace of pheasants for the assistant head brewer, he'd show you how they make the stuff if you asked him.'

Ten minutes later as I hitched the two-wheel trailer to his car he placed a pair of colourful cock birds into the boot.

'Tell him they've been hanging a week,' he said with his usual wry grin, and Sylvia gave me a sweet smile from her bedroom window as I drove off. Like me she realised her father was invincible. Just like most breweries, William Hancock's appeared as an antiquity that had survived for centuries. Its uneven mass of buildings, covering its own water wells near the famous River Taff, belched out daily from its shining coppers the distinct fumes of boiled barley, malt and hops. I paused to look at the giant kettles as men, stripped to the waist, shovelled out the steaming spent petals and grains. Basically the method has remained unchanged since brewing began. The infused liquid known as wort had been drained to the large stainless steel fermenting vats where yeast was added, and a fine creamy head grew on the surface as alcohol was created to finally earn the name beer.

The recipient of the pheasants was gratefully helpful to me as I bombarded him with questions.

'It all starts from these little blighters,' he said delving his fingers into a small container of barley grains. 'Like that they're all starch, but we have to convert them into sugar for malting purposes, so we germinate the bounders, we spray them with water in our malthouse and in seventy-two hours

they produce roots and a little top shoot, then we roast them into malt.'

'What about the hops?' I asked. 'Where do they come into it?'

His angular features broke into a broad smile. 'Ah, the biggest fallacy of the brewing game, nothing to do with the gravity as most people believe. They're a flower you know, and the petals, which are called bracts in the trade, contain a chemical which preserves and flavours the beer and most important, provides the bouquet.'

I followed him into the fermenting rooms where the hop odour pervaded all powerful, and I sensed the devotion and magnetism to his skilled trade as he looked upon his various lakes of beer with pride.

He turned to face me with a smile on the catwalk between two vats. 'One of our competitors lost a night watchman a few years back. They reckon he was taking a sip out of these things when he fell in and drowned. What a way to go, aye.'

We eventually arrived back at my father-in-law's car with its loaded trailer of steaming pigs' food.

'Please convey my thanks for the pheasants,' said the brewer, and I headed for the Six Bells with a little more knowledge of the trade, that constantly beckoned to me.

'Fine chap, isn't he,' said Bob Styles, as we unloaded the hops into a brick store shed near the pigsty. 'Used to drive up to Burton-on-Trent regularly for him before the war for fresh yeast. They got to change it every so often because the beer gets too familiar with it.'

'I wish I could become a little more familiar with him,' said Sylvia in the doorway, obviously ready for a second attempt at a run in the Morris.

The vale of Glamorgan was more magical than usual that late summer afternoon as the little car raced through the maze of lanes to appear suddenly in picturesque villages and on again into the deep green of its glorious countryside. With the hood down we experienced the exhilaration of a sports car as the warm wind caressed our faces, and the whole situation smacked of a fantasy that only films depicted in those spartan post-war days. Suddenly as I took a severe humpback bridge far too fast, the car became momentarily airborne as her wheels left the road to land with a bone-jarring thump on the road at the opposite side of the river. There followed an ominous hiss of air as the steering-wheel pulled violently to indicate a front wheel puncture.

'Damn it,' I said, kicking the offending wheel hub. 'I haven't got a spare, that's in for repair also, it's been there a week, I completely forgot about it.' My savage emotional outburst was soon rewarded with an intense pain in the sole of my foot which caused me to limp.

Sylvia's knowledge of the Vale quickly established the nearest garage to involve us in a round journey of more than three miles which I covered painfully on foot and heel, while she manipulated the wheel. Three hours later in a blood-red sunset we headed back along the coast road for Penmark as I nursed my ever-expanding foot and Sylvia handled the car in a far more sensible way than I would.

At Aberthaw we gazed across a flat calm sea to the stark outline of the Somerset coast, and into the majestic panorama sailed the White Funnel line paddle-steamer *Cardiff Queen*. Just like a water bus of the Bristol Channel she and her beautiful sisters plied the seaway from Lundy to the Avon with precision timing. To people on both coasts, English and Welsh, they were a fact of life; now alas they are extinct. At that moment, as I became enchanted with the romantic situation, the choice of prose for my proposal went utterly haywire.

'I earned quite a good commission last week,' I stammered with a mixture of pain and embarrassment. 'Do you fancy a day trip on her down to Ilfracombe tomorrow or would you rather get engaged.'

She smiled back unperturbed and then turned her head towards the steamer. 'Well it all depends on who you want to marry, doesn't it, me or the *Cardiff Queen*.'

I slouched back into my seat cursing the choice of my utterly bungled proposal, but that night as I lay in bed with my throbbing foot protected by a cardboard box from the weight of the bedclothes, I knew the paddle steamer would sail without us the following morning in favour of Sylvia – and the Bells which also summoned me.

2 · Scrumpy

WITH THE exception of my new shoes, our wedding in September 1957 went off quite well. They were a black pair offered forlornly in a lingering summer sale for thirty shillings. While suffering my life-long disease of limited financial resources I eagerly purchased the bargain to match my new groom's grey suit. Through my own neglect the Morris Tourer had become quite unreliable and at Sylvia's insistence I arranged to spend my last night as a bachelor at Aubrey Bower's cottage next door to the pub. As I sat on the foot of the bed at the dawn of the great day, with the ravages of far too many stag-nights affecting my head, Aubrey's sister Lily entered my room with a breakfast of two boiled eggs and three thick rounds of bread and butter. A wave of nausea rose from my stomach as she placed the tray on the marble-top wash-stand with a maternal smile, despite her spinsterhood.

'There you are, Derek, that will see you through to the reception, you'll need a bit of packing for the ordeal.'

Her ill-chosen words of comfort belied her wonderful character and I knew my refusal of the breakfast would upset her so I hastily swept it off the plate into my suitcase as soon as she left the room. I shall never forget Sylvia's face when they re-appeared in our hotel room that night as we prepared for bed. But back to my footwear.

'Did you notice their smiles?' said Bill, my best man, as the photographs were being taken. I shook my head. 'Well, look at the bottoms of your shoes,' he continued, with a broad smile. On the near perfect cream-coloured soles a vivid black marker pen had inscribed SALE PRICE 30/-. Bill slapped my shoulder, 'The whole church could see them when you knelt at the chancel, I looked behind to a sea of suppressed laughter when I heard the giggles.' I realised then that my short journey from the cottage to the church had done little to erase my bargain price. My father-in-law looked completely out of character in a hired morning suit that was rather on the small side, and he hastily discarded his top hat when Sylvia said, 'It's stuck on top of your head like Stan Laurel's bowler, Dad, for goodness sake carry it for the photographs.'

During the reception he revealed his true intention of my future, but in a concealed manner. 'Had a letter from the National Trade Development Association this morning,' he whispered loudly, as the best man read the greetings. 'They're backed by the breweries to raise the standard of pub keeping, they're running one of their training courses at Cardiff Technical College next year.' His eyes searched my face for the tone of my response. 'I'm too old in the tooth for it, but it could be useful to you if ever you thought of going in for a place of your own.' As the reception progressed he continually returned to the subject at regular intervals until his usual persuasive power won the day, and I agreed to enlist for the three-month course during the following year.

Fortunately I had the type of sales job that was paid only on results which made me rather a master of my own destiny, and I was able to attend the twice-weekly lectures with minimum inconvenience to my earning potential. Every facet of the industry was covered by the various specialists, from brewing to carpet care, from book-keeping to catering, all combined with visits to various relevant establishments and practical demonstrations, such as cocktail making by the celebrated barman of a world-famous London hotel.

Finally, in December 1960, we sat the day-long examination, and I was delighted to receive a credit diploma some months later, during a lavish luncheon at the Cardiff Royal Hotel.

Theoretically I was fully qualified to manage and work at every function of public house operation, but on beer-keeping at least, I felt my father-in-law still had the edge over me with his old and tried practical methods. Following my success I decided to join the 'Trade' but definitely from the right side of the bar as a company representative. That could be the change I'm looking for, I thought. A let-yourself-go type of selling job. A wonderful adventure. A glorious departure from my enforced clinical image. A leave of absence from the professional buyer.

My future customers, I envisaged, would be bosom-proud, motherly landladies who would fall for my youthful charm to swell my order-book with success. After months of fruitless searching, the columns of a national daily newspaper finally revealed a breakthrough which read 'Cider company requires sales representative for South Wales area.'

The interview passed victoriously for me in the meeting room of a Cardiff hotel. 'You'll spend a week at our factory in Somerset,' said a rosy-faced sales manager. 'See how it's made, sort o' thing, product knowledge, you've got to know what you're selling to obtain orders, it's not just a round of drinks, and on your way, you know.'

No one wished to bother with me during the first day except a friendly lorry driver. 'Yer lookin' quite cheesed off me ol' pal,' he said with a broad smile. 'Fancy a trip down to Avonmouth? I gotta get a load of apples from the dock.'

'Avonmouth?' I said with an obvious puzzled expression. 'From the docks?'

'That's right me old fruit, French apples, bin a lousy Somerset crop this year, got to buy off the froggies we 'ave.'

I suppose they have commercial immunity for such a ruse, I thought, but what a swindle to the thousands of innocent scrumpy drinkers, who would be too numb to detect the difference in any case.

'Why don't they sell it as French cider?' I shouted across to the driver as the truck rolled along the glorious Somerset countryside.

'They'd never sell a drop,' answered the driver. 'Connoisseurs of Somerset cider wouldn't touch it. Same thing goes for the Hereford scrumpy wallahs, only Hereford apples for their plonk.' He turned to face me, causing my right foot to apply an imaginary brake. 'Mind you, they're having half this cargo, so all the silly buggers will be swallowing Hereford and Somerset, French scrumpy like, bloody laugh innit, but I s'pose it's the way they make it what counts like.'

During my second day I was invited to attend the daily tasting ritual. With a sense of urgency of being summoned like Cabinet Ministers to the Prime Minister, six senior members of the staff converged on the tasting room at precisely ten-thirty. Five small glasses were placed before each of us. They were identified in alphabetical order and our own brew was concealed within them. I tried to mimic the six tasters as they began their daily ritual. No wine from the finest vineyard of France could receive such treatment. They looked, they smelled, they tasted and they spat before writing down their judgement. I fought hard to make an intelligent assessment, but the five humble glasses of scrumpy looked, smelled and tasted exactly the same.

I guessed my choices in order of preference before a disdainful audience, to place our own brew last. Lady Luck spurned me for the remainder of that week when my best attempt could only guess my own firm into third place, but I did learn a little of the art of cider-making, and on the following Monday I met my field trainer at a local brewery, who were also our main stockists. He ushered me past the deafening sound of bottling machines into a small office where I was introduced to Arthur, the bottle hall manager.

'Pleased to meet you,' he shouted above the bedlam noise of the plant. 'Fancy a drop of breakfast?' I glanced at my watch as he dragged in a crate of Guinness. It was nine-thirty. We left an hour later decidedly light-headed.

'Hard going this time of the morning,' said my red-faced tutor, who, I noticed, had managed to force down ten bottles with relish. 'Got to watch your intake in this job,' he continued, as we headed for the workingmen's clubs of the Rhondda Valley. 'Occupational hazard, you have to treat booze with respect, it's seen off many a good man.'

The breathalyser was unheard of and one had to be a rip-roaring drunk before the police called out their doctor, who would ask you only to touch your nose with the index finger and walk a chalk line along the floor of the police station before he passed judgement.

The hazard was recognised by the aristocrat companies of the trade who provided a chauffeur, but the profits of the humble scrumpy would not permit such a luxury.

We arrived at a large single-storey shed on a patch of waste ground. A highly polished brass plate on the front door read KARL MARX SOCIAL CLUB. A dejected steward jerked his thumb toward a door marked SECRETARY. 'You'll find Lenin in there,' he said.

The interior of the secretary's office was another world in comparison to the spartan club outside. No boardroom of a multi-national company could equal its splendour. The great man sat at the end of a magnificent oak table with the *Daily Worker* spread before him at the sports page, his blue-scarred features portrayed a history of many years at the coal face. His jerky breathing indicated dust-polluted lungs. His arthritic deformed index finger pointed at me after the introductions had been completed.

'There's good trade to be had in the club, boyo, twenty barrels a week. Scrumpy is scrumpy as far as I'm concerned, so whoever looks after us the best gets the business see.' He smiled shamelessly throughout his capitalist foray. 'And don't come to see me again without a large rum, the steward should have told you so.'

The steward later informed us that Lenin ruled the club with an iron fist and no one had the courage to confront him.

Six calls later found me with a slight slur in my speech while my well-seasoned colleague suffered only a deeper shade of red as he constantly reminded me of the pitfalls of over-indulgence. I soon realised that if one had the stamina the job could be a boozer's dream. Contrary to the sales manager very little selling expertise was required in favour of a good bar personality, the ability to dig deep for the never-ending rounds of drinks and a constant supply of dripmats. The seventh call, a Conservative Club, proved to be a pleasant change from bar propping.

'Am I glad to see you,' said a worried steward to my tutor. 'I phoned up your office and they said you were in the area.'

'What's the trouble?' asked my seasoned mentor.

'Clear cider,' answered the steward, 'as clear as champagne.'

'Oh my God,' said my colleague, 'I'll get on to the factory right away.'

The steward noticed my puzzled expression. 'They won't touch clear scrumpy in the Valleys, they reckon there's no body in it. It's got to be like pea soup.'

My tutor returned from the phone. 'We've got to meet the head cider-maker at Cardiff station, he's travelling over with some conditioner to make it thick.'

My fuzzy brain became even more boggled. All the advertising stressed Cool, Clear Somerset Cider, which it was, yet the head man was speeding towards us at that very moment to destroy its clarity.

Three hours later we were back in the cellar of the Conservative Club to witness the great man perform his skills on the row of offending barrels. From a large holdall he produced several quart bottles of a glutinous brown liquid.

'Remove all the spile bungs, steward, there's a good fellow,' he said, in a cultured voice of authority. I was later to discover that all head brewers and cider-makers spoke in the same tone.

Half a bottle of the vile-looking concoction was poured through each hole and the bung replaced.

'Right,' said the cider-maker, 'shake hell out of the casks.'

I shrank back in horror with visions of my father-in-law's cellar where he even forbade loud talking as part of his humour. 'Try a pint now, steward,' he commanded.

There was a breathless silence. He held a glass of murky liquid to the light with a sparkle of triumph in his eyes. 'That's it, boys, you've done it, just like pea soup.'

The cider-maker suddenly went into spasms of laughter. 'Do you know, chaps, throughout this exercise I've had one of those sensations of having been here before, and I jolly well have. Many years ago, I was under brewer at the Rhymney Brewery just up the Valley, and it was this club who complained of cloudy beer, so I rushed here to clear it with finings. It just proves', he went on, 'we are a nation of sight drinkers. Providing it's fresh I could blindfold your beer and cider drinkers and they could never tell the clarity. The additives are tasteless and the end result is purely cosmetic.' He pointed across to the beer stillages. 'It's a miracle how you keep any good ale, steward. Cider and beer don't live well together, and it's the ale that suffers from the wild yeasts of the cider.'

I later discovered, when I kept my own pub, that a slow-selling cask of beer would in fact develop more clarity, and, while looking a perfect pint on the counter, it had most certainly lost its nutty flavour and been replaced by a rather sharp acid taste. But as our brewer had observed, no one complained of a clear beer!

It was well into the evening before we returned our man to Cardiff station, after a mission completed – the club steward was happily serving cloudy cider and clear beer. He wouldn't let us depart without 'one for the road' in the station refreshment room, where he continued his interesting sight drinking theory. 'There was no clear beer two hundred years ago – just as well that they drank from mugs before brewers used finings.'

'What are finings?' asked my colleague.

'Fish, it comes from the Japanese sturgeon. Egg white will do the same thing though.'

'How does it work?' I asked.

'Not the way you'd imagine,' said the brewer. 'If you were to look at a glass-ended cask of unfined beer you would see millions of molecules of unfermented matter, all restless and continually moving, keeping the ale cloudy. Now the finings, when added, don't drag these little gubbins to the bottom of the cask, which is an obvious conclusion. They neutralise the matter which then sinks to the belly of the barrel, and the beer becomes clear. Of course,' he laughed, 'given ten years or so, it'll be all keg and the art of beer-keeping will be forgotten.'

I quite enjoyed my cider selling job, despite the constant battle to retain my sobriety, but without the stonewall excuse of the breathalyser to shield me, it was extremely difficult.

I worked at the Six Bells two nights a week and on one momentous occasion my father-in-law entrusted me to take charge when, for the first time in his life, he took a short holiday at Bournemouth. He phoned me each night to know how the beer was behaving. Had I fed the dogs correctly and had the big sow farrowed yet? He had some of the finest pigs in the area, but all inveterate drunkards, weaned from an early age on barrel drainings.

It was quite an eye-opener to see them take their daily tipple, then stagger around the sty before going into a deep snoring sleep. My orders were to make sure the large white sow had a good swig when she went into labour.

'She won't know she's had them,' he told me.

Susan, my five-year-old daughter, heard his instructions and kept a constant vigil for the great event. I had half a dozen lunchtime customers when she rushed into the bar. 'Dad,' she said in a breathless voice, 'the old sow's ready for her beer.'

There were raised eyebrows from all my customers, who were complete strangers, hardly believing that my charming little daughter was referring to a pig.

The weeks that followed were most certainly turbulent. My wife entered hospital for the complicated birth of my son, Stewart. My company offered an area management position which would involve moving away, and my ever-impulsive father-in-law tendered his notice of retirement to the brewery.

'I've told the gaffer that I want you to have it,' he continued, when I returned from the hospital one evening. The gaffer was the managing director of Hancock's Brewery.

'Well you picked a damn fine time to pack it in,' I said in temper. 'I'm not sure if I want it, and Sylvia won't have much time for it with a new baby to look after, besides I've had an offer of promotion from my company.'

He looked down at his feet, like an admonished schoolboy. 'I always wanted to keep it in the family, didn't have much chance with only a daughter, till you came along.' He looked up with a sparkle in his eyes, 'I told the brewery about your diploma.'

I snapped back at him, 'Why couldn't you wait until I had a chance to talk it over with Sylvia, she might be all for it when the baby is a little older.'

'Doctor's orders, son, I've had a couple of queer turns recently, it's my ticker.'

The following evening I tried to explain the situation to my

wife. 'What shall I do?' I pleaded. 'Shall I take the pub, take promotion or stay as I am?'

I became ashamed of my action, it was unfair to place her in such a position. Later that night, just after closing time, I sat around the dying embers of the bar fireplace with my in-laws. After ten years of just a casual acquaintance with the place I felt that it was part of me, or I was part of it. I wondered how they felt after a third of a century. As I studied the changing patterns of fire on the spent logs, my mind raced for the decision that I knew they wanted to hear. The old inn seemed to wrap itself around me in persuasion.

'I'll take it over,' I said with a feeling of release from my tormented mind.

His face beamed, 'You'll have to see the gaffer to be short-listed and all that nonsense, but you're past the post. He promised me that. February the seventeenth you take over, at the next Brewsters' Session.'

I jumped from my chair to stand over him. 'You crafty old devil, you had it planned all along.'

He smiled back with misted eyes of gratitude. 'What do you mean, there'll be a hundred or so after this place, you're lucky to have me pulling the strings for you.'

The following morning as I quickly scanned the daily newspaper over a cup of breakfast tea a small heading caught my attention: MOTORISTS BEWARE – THE BREATHALYSER COMETH. I read the details and closed the paper savagely. The Six Bells was essentially a car trade pub.

3 · My Pub

WILLIAM HANCOCK & COMPANY, BREWERS SINCE
1750, read the goldleaf sign over the brewery
entrance. The coppers were open and the air was
heavy with the strong odours of malt and spent hops. It was a
picture that had barely changed in centuries. Even a horse-
drawn dray prepared to load for the local deliveries as its two
massive shires dipped their graceful heads into their nosebags.
Steam-pipes seemed to be leaking little wisps of white vapour
everywhere, amidst a hive of industry. Large wooden barrels
came out onto the loading bay with a dull thud as if by magic
and their shining new aluminium counterparts clattered out

with a metallic ring – all to be manhandled onto the waiting drays with the ease of a bale of sponges. I was to learn later that nothing could supersede this wonderful Egyptian invention of four thousand years ago for transporting liquids: the barrel. Despite my salesman's confidence, I confronted the great man with some trepidation. My father-in-law regarded him highly on all counts except the rent.

'Watch him on that,' was his fond briefing. 'It was ten shillings for years. He tried and tried to raise it to a pound. Used to call here in his chauffeur-driven car. I'd get him mellow on a couple of jars. The missus would make him a game pie, then I'd take him for a stroll down to the livestock, collect him a dozen eggs off the nests and away he would go. "Bob Styles," he'd say, as he was getting into the car, "you'll make this brewery bankrupt." '

The gaffer sized me up quickly before extending his arm towards my chair. It was an obvious foregone conclusion that the pub was mine by the tone of the interview, yet I felt that my personal qualities had little bearing on his choice. It was decidedly my father-in-law who had pulled the strings that would allow me to succeed over the small army of other applicants.

'You're picking a hard man to follow in more ways than one,' he said with a smile. 'Used to play with the blighter in the brewery rugby side, strongest chap I can ever recall. We've got a file of customer complaints on him, mainly regarding his personality, which is rather brusque, but as a country inn-keeper he's superb. It's a totally different world from the town publican. There's much more involvement in village life with all classes. You're an integral part of the community just as much as the church is.' He began to thumb through the file on his desk. 'I've little doubt that your father-in-law has not briefed you in resisting a rent increase?' I could feel the flush of my face as the truth willed out, and I made a feeble nod of my head with a half smile. 'Well it's beyond a joke now, Mr Brock. That miserable, ridiculous little pittance, despite constant inflation, has remained the same for the last twenty years.' His face mellowed into a pleasant smile. 'You might inherit the crafty old blighter's pub, Mr Brock, but I'm damned sure you'll pay a sensible rent for it. What do you say to five pounds a week?'

I wasn't in the least concerned over the massive increase – it was still well below the average rate for a tenancy – but the humiliation of admitting defeat to my Fagin-styled conniver back at the pub was going to be a bitter pill.

It was all good fun and I think a draw would have been the best result for the twenty-year-old wrangle.

Times were changing fast, however, for the once-isolated country pub since the growth of car ownership, and the breweries were eager to exploit the increased revenue from properties that had barely covered their costs in the past.

The Six Bells was no exception as the gaffer pointed out to me. 'No doubt you'll put your recent successful diploma to good use and I'd like to see you venture more into catering.'

Three weeks later I was informed by letter that I had been successful in my application, subject to obtaining a licence from the next Brewsters' Sessions at Barry Magistrates Court.

From then on I felt like a hardened criminal seeking a licence to murder. For a number of weeks preceding the day of the transfer I was interrogated by a sergeant of the Glamorgan Constabulary. I am convinced that they considered only God to be a fit and proper person to hold a pub licence.

With a heavy heart and considerable trepidation, I tendered my notice to my cider company; I was about to foresake my freedom of the road to become a prisoner behind the bar.

The great day was 17 February 1965 – the Brewsters' Sessions. I listened as various brewery representatives applied for the renewal of their pub licences in block, followed by the owners of free houses, secretaries of clubs and proprietors of off-licence shops. It was all so formal with the chief inspector of police making occasional prudent remarks regarding the conduct of certain properties followed by warnings from the chairman of the court about the future behaviour of the licensee concerned.

There was one strong objection to a renewal, and following some considerable debate over the publican's persistance in serving after hours, his licence was refused. I couldn't help feeling pity for the man and his family; from that moment they were without a job and a home. I resolved that I would not leave the Six Bells in that manner, and while my resolution was to earn me a bad name for being a time fanatic, I stuck to my principles throughout, with the recollection of that miserable publican firmly embossed on my memory.

My heartbeat increased as the court orderly said 'Transfers' and my name was shouted across the court room.

'Any reason why the applicant should not hold this licence?' said the clerk.

'None,' replied the inspector, and from that moment I was an innkeeper.

The inspector concluded with generous praise for the manner in which my father-in-law had conducted the premises during thirty years, and wished him a happy retirement. As we left the court he said, 'Let that be a lesson. If you keep to the law you'll be unpopular with the customers and if you oblige the customers you'll be out of favour with the police.'

A normal transfer is a very traumatic time for both parties. They have to start at daybreak, sometimes earlier, to complete the takeover by morning opening time.

As one removal van delivers another takes away, a rapid stock check has to be taken, agreed, and paid for, and if the new tenants are also coming from another pub, a chain reaction can arise. In our case, my father-in-law had been quietly moving to his retirement cottage for some time, so there was little hassle. The brewery representative had me sign three copies of my contract and insisted on my newly painted name plate being fixed over the front door in readiness for opening time. There was nothing really new to the situation. I had been in close contact with the inn for ten years, but I think I enjoyed the egoism of being called its landlord.

The till suffered badly the first day with a free drink to all my regulars. It suffered the second day in reverse, chargeable drinks but few customers. Morning trade was miserable to say the least with the exception of Sundays, which was by then legal in certain parts of Wales.

The cleaning took about two hours and half a tin of Brasso. I'm sure my father-in-law made a fetish of the stuff. He even polished the toilet pipes to a rich copper lustre. The local wags said that whilst his catering standards of unvarying hot pasties left a lot to be desired, he did possess the coveted good bog diploma.

My regulars were the local racehorse owners. There were two notables stables, with winners of quite important races to their credit. For two hours they would talk horses while the eager receptive ears of a potential starry-eyed punter would strain for a tip at the end of the bar.

If the truth were known, their most enthusiastic advice would be no more than 'He's trying today, so have sixpence each way on him', but these were the 'county' people, a race apart from any others. They were a world unto themselves, a clique who allow no intrusion into their way of life. Money and possessions were not necessarily their criterion, but breeding. I have seen wealthy outsiders attempt to gate-crash their company at the bar, only to receive the politest of rebuffs.

My father-in-law was the son of a gamekeeper. From the cradle he had learnt to doff his hat. He was a true county servant, a countryman through and through, and they loved him for it. But it requires inherent training to acquire the subservience they expect, and being a townie, I didn't possess it.

When my licence was just a month old came the acid test. It was a bitter March day and my county regulars were encircled around the glorious but expensive roaring coal fire when a tap on the widow drew our attention. She was the very attractive Lady Cleaver, resplendent in her immaculate habit astride her black hunter.

'Can't come in,' she shouted, 'The bounder won't be tethered, must be held.'

The female member of my customers spoke to my father-in-
law who had just arrived on his regular daily visit.

'Now Robert, who will be the gentleman and hold Lady
Cleaver's horse, you or Derek?'

This was true county talk, not will you but who will; I was
determined not to take on his subservience to these people. He
was sixty plus with a heart condition and retired, but in their
eyes still a faithful servant. I was the young townie who had to
be house-trained.

'I think your party can provide truer gentlemen than we are,'
I answered with a smile.

'Bloody clever diplomacy that, old boy,' said a male member
of the party. 'A politician you should have been, not a publican. Damn it, I'll be the gentleman, but only for five minutes.
It's brass monkey weather out there.'

It was to be the first of many mild rebellions with the county
set, but I'm sure they accepted it in good faith as modern-day
socialist decadence on my part.

It was ten year since I first helped my father-in-law to horse a
cask at shoulder level, but thankfully through the fear of heart
strain and hernias he had progressed to beer engines. The
pipeline was quite short, about twenty feet at the most, and
the beer held on to its excellent reputation.

During the latter part of my first week I went through the
pipe-cleaning ritual according to his training. No patent
chemicals for him. 'Ruins beer,' he'd stress. His method was
painstaking but extremely effective. Ordinary household soda
was the cleaning agent; a one-pound packet dissolved in two
gallons of boiling water was pulled into the system and left to
soak for an hour. After this was drawn off, looking like a
reasonably attractive bitter ale, a pound block of rock salt was
also dissolved in two gallons of boiling water to soak in the
system for another hour. When that was drawn off, my instructions were to keep pulling fresh water through 'until your

arm aches'. The final test was to taste the water, and then pull the beer through.

I had completed the first phase, leaving the system to soak in the soda water while I delivered a firkin of Guinness to one of the racing stables. The owner was confident that her horses' success was due to a daily tipple of the famous stout with their oats, not to mention the healthy bloom of the head lad who administered the tonic.

It was opening time when I returned to be confronted by a very distressed wife.

'What on earth have you done to the beer?' she said. 'That horrible tramp from the old quarry called in for a pint, Dad would never serve him, but I was afraid of him, so I did.'

I noticed the nearly full pint of rather dubious ale on the counter. 'You didn't serve him that did you?'

'Yes, and he ran out saying I was trying to kill him.'

I burst into laughter. 'Well that's really an ill wind blowing good. I wondered how on earth I was going to dissuade him from calling here because he's a real nasty character, and you've done it with a pint of household soda water.'

More of my father-in-law's exiles were to re-appear as the weeks wore on and, despite his reputation, I felt he had good reason to 'freeze' some of them away. But I decided to accept all comers under my roof in the true tradition of the hostelry.

4 · The Villagers

Hᴵˢ ꜰᴀᴄᴇ was new to me. 'Pint of PA,' he said curtly. He was one of several new customers drawn to the Six Bells by the change of its landlord. The villagers had long since passed their judgement on me, dismissive or tolerant, and whilst I enjoyed the increased trade of inquisitive new-comers I suffered the uncomfortable experience of being on trial as their searching eyes followed my every move. The fresh kil of lively pale ale was at its best and my chest swelled with proud confidence as I pulled slowly on the pump to produce a deep amber-coloured pint with the clarity of champagne. The man studied it intently while I waited for payment. If he is a sight drinker, I thought, perhaps he is entranced with its superb appearance, but wait until he tastes its exquisite flavour, unique to Hancock's brewers.

My fantasy was short-lived when he pointed at the slowly diminishing creamy head.

'Reckon there's room for a double whisky in there?' he said in a questioning tone.

'Certainly, sir,' I replied, in all innocence, as I began to hold a goblet to the whisky optic.

'Well don't bother,' he continued with a smile of sarcasm. 'Just put the same amount of beer in the glass.' I fought to control my acid glare and clenched teeth as I returned his overflowing pint to the counter. His right hand took on a psychological tremor as he raised the beer to his lips before the audience that he had created. An ominous sound of spilt beer splashing to the counter revealed a deficiency of more than his initial devious complaint.

Victory of the round was obviously mine, as the trouble-maker flushed with embarrassment, and the final death-blow to his injured pride came when one of the villagers offered him a straw from the counter dispenser.

The subtle action of support for me revealed the strong underlying communal spirit of the village. He took exception to a stranger entering his pub to create a nuisance. There was no loyalty to me, I suspect; more an objection to the rude intrusion of his established way of life. On the surface the locals appeared extremely independent, but how they rallied to any just cause. One middle-aged inhabitant, for example, spent most of the year in virtual isolation at his remote cottage to appear early on each Christmas morning with a large basket of wines and spirits. He called at every house in the village to offer his festive drink, and how he ever succeeded in returning to his seclusion still remains a mystery. Most of the adult population quietly cycled to and from their various occupations sometimes covering a round journey of more than ten miles, and once the school bus had collected its children the village took on its intense character of absolute serenity.

I shall always treasure a magical memory when I finished my chores early one fine spring morning. With the exception of my footsteps, the village seemed to doze in a perfection of silence as I strolled down its single street towards the humpback bridge at Kenson where old Mr Taylor worked relentlessly on his mainly futile inventions. He was a newcomer of some thirty years' standing, a retired Royal Air Force instructor who would end his days at his cosy cottage alongside the lazy river Thaw. He hailed me from the doorway of his lean-to workshop. My nostrils took in the fusty romantic mixed odours of paint, paraffin and woodshavings as I took a seat among the confusion of his creative hoard.

'What do you think of this?' he said with a slight trace of an English accent. It was a long brass tube with a curtain ring at one end attached to a length of string. 'That's for picking up adders, that is,' he said proudly. 'There's quite a lot over there by the marsh. I've been practising on 'em, just get the ring past their head I do, then pull tight on the string and I got him.' I smiled weakly as I mused on his logic, but I enjoyed the simple atmosphere beneath that ancient stone-tiled roof with its woodworm-ridden trusses of oak.

Under the single-arched bridge nearby I saw the crouched figure of a man I knew to be a trout tickler. With his arm submerged to the elbow his fingers deftly caressed the belly of his victim into a submissive trance when he would grasp it from the water. Further up stream on my circular journey where moorhens popped out from holes in the bank I came to a deep, still patch of river where I sat to gaze at its sheer tranquillity through an opening of bullrushes. Suddenly the mirror surface was broken by a V-shaped ripple as the cheeky, whiskered head of an otter came onto the scene. Sadly these creatures have been hunted to near extinction and I treasure dearly in my mind that momentary glimpse.

As I crossed the road from the back field to the pub a matronly female approached me with a positive gait. Her two

English Springers dragged her towards me in untrained behaviour. I recognised her as one of the recent additions to the village.

'Ah, Mr Brock,' she said in a clipped voice. 'I intended to call on you in the near future but there's no time like the present is there?' I succumbed to her headmistress presence. 'The village is quite decadent really. I and a few of the more recent additions to the community have formed the nucleus of a society to enhance its artistic and social qualities.' She stooped to pick up a flattened cigarette packet from the gutter. 'Dispose of that please, Mr Brock, it more than likely emanated from the pub, we must condition ourselves for entry into the Best Kept Village Competition.' I accepted the litter in stunned obedience as I gazed longingly at the sanctuary of the Bells, so tantalisingly near, but she had not finished with me. 'We've decided for obvious reasons that our local innkeeper should join the committee, so I extend the invitation, the next meeting is at my house, 8 pm on Friday.'

'They want to put Penmark on the map so it seems,' I said to Sylvia jokingly as I repeated the incident in the kitchen. 'It wouldn't be a bad thing for the Bells, I suppose. The Best Kept Village usually attracts a constant trickle of viewers.'

She paused in her kneading of a cake mix. 'Be careful you don't fall out with the real villagers,' she replied as the back of her flour-covered hand relieved an obvious tickle on the tip of her nose. 'They don't like change, you know. These new people should consider their feelings.'

But with the moral support of our local farmer, who had also been enlisted in the movement, we set about our first task of rescuing the dilapidated school hall from its years of idle retirement. Only the oldest inhabitants could recall its school service days, but Sylvia remembered its final use as a wartime venue for the weekly village dance. Grey garlands of dustladen cobwebs hung from the exposed pine roof trusses where once children's voices echoed. Countless knots in the floorboards protruded hard and shining like so many foot bunions where generations of young feet had worn away the soft wood around them. Thick layers of whitewash and distemper curled back from the walls like ancient scrolls, and the once ornate wainscot carried the ominous evidence of a mammoth wood-worm colony. We stood in awe near the Victorian black cast-iron fireplace, and as our faces met we burst into laughter.

'Where the hell do we start?' said the farmer, wiping tears from his eyes. 'Sounded all very well after a couple of sherries in her cosy living room the other night, but the only answer for this place is to pull it down and start again.' One enterprising newcomer had planned just that some years previous, working ceaselessly on fund-raising schemes such as the largest carnival and fête the Vale had seen, but there was a difference of opinion between the village saviours, and the locals looked on in humorous silence as the whole affair disbanded.

'Antiquity is what we're after,' said our Chairwoman. 'Not a modern social centre in a medieval village.' I suppose she was right, but with a limited labour force comprising me and the farmer during our precious free time the prospect of a rejuven-ated village hall appeared rather remote.

'Well, let's make a start,' said my colleague tearing away a panel of wainscot amidst a cloud of woodworm dust.

We had cleared and burned one wall of the ancient carpeting when the vicar arrived. He fanned the acrid interior with his black trilby as he peered into the hall. The building was owned by the church, and he was its guardian.

'Where are you taking that?' he coughed.

'Just around the back, vicar,' lied the quick-thinking culprit. 'Only fit for the fire mind you,' he added. 'It's full of worm.'

'No doubt,' replied the vicar as he peered closely at the dart-hole surface of a panel. 'But it came originally from the church and it may be still consecrated, so don't dispose of it until I make inquiries.'

'Well half of it's gone to hell blessed or not,' whispered the farmer as the vicar left the hall. We both suffered a few nail-biting days until he returned with the news that we could dispose of the woodworm sanctuary in a fit and proper manner.

'So what better Christian end than cremation,' I proposed.

'Pity we haven't a larger fireplace,' said the farmer as we stacked the final panel in the hall centre.

'I wonder what's behind that little grate,' I asked. 'Just look at the size of the chimney breast, it's massive.' My sentence had barely finished when his sledgehammer began to attack the cast iron savagely. As we pulled the frontal away a ton of loose rubble spewed over the hearth to reveal a beautiful inglenook fireplace crowned with a huge oak beam. It seemed to swell with exhilaration and gratitude for its new-found liberty and the building immediately reclaimed its historical elegance, as we stoked the doomed wainscot into its hungry jaws. Our discovery aroused a wave of interest from the reluctant villagers who were quickly enlisted to the cause when their curiosity brought them to the scene.

Some months later when the hall was an established focal point of the village I was approached by the master of the county Bassett Hounds. Ironically he was the person who worked so hard on the first village hall scheme; a magnificent character who commanded the highest respect from all sections of rural society.

'We're hunting this area next Saturday, Derek,' he began in his usual polite manner. 'Do you think you could provide our breakfast down at the hall? Cold buffet and beer would be fine.'

It was to be the first of many conflicts within myself on the delicate subject of hunting. While I am far from a fervent abolitionist of field sports, my conscience has always mildly decreed that it is morally wrong to hunt for pleasure. So weak was the division within me that I went on several shoots with father-in-law on the pretext of hunting essential food, but I could never face my victims on the dinner plate. On reflection perhaps I was not the proper person to run a country inn, for the landlord supplying his stirrup cups to a colourful hunt is a

centuries-old scene. But how cruel can be hypocrisy as I prepared my hunters' feast that chill Saturday morning when the huge criss-cross pile of burning elm logs spat out their welcome warmth to the band of men who had walked with their baying hounds since the crack of dawn. I never dreamt such a postcard scene could be so factual as the rosy-faced group in their black hats and scarlet coats took their feast with relish before the wonderful lighting effect of that magnificent fireplace.

My next role was Father Christmas at the first annual children's party. I assumed that my disguise and change of voice was foolproof as I rang my bell to distribute the gifts, but daughter Susan destroyed my image in one simple sentence of 'Thank you, Dad' as she accepted her present. A dedicated band of workers laboured ceaselessly in the old building to complete its rescue, and today it enjoys a lively activity as a true village hall. But our leader's dream of the Best Kept Village never materialised. It would require a complete population change, for I could not visualise any of the sensitive villagers risking the humorous ridicule of their neighbours as they collected the odd cigarette packet off the street.

The contrast of rural and urban pubs, I discovered, was blatantly obvious as far as the clientele were concerned. The village inn could lose a customer for a mere unchosen word from the landlord, or even his off-day facial expression. One local reappeared at the Six Bells after an absence of ten years. Choosing the quiet morning session for his return, he gave me a sheepish glance as he ordered his pint. His eyes expressed an emotional pleasure as they slowly scanned the room.

'Never cared for that other place really,' was his first remark after sampling his pint with a critical tasting routine. 'Sides that, I'm not too clever on the old bike these days, specially when I've had a couple too many.' He tapped his unlit Woodbine on the packet. 'Only a little tiff with Bob your father-in-law, it was, 'bout the dartboard, I remember. He reckoned I commandeered it all night, and that was it,' he concluded, nodding his head toward the next village. 'I been going over there ever since.' He walked over to the wooden armchair at the fireplace. 'This was my chair, course, I been coming here for nigh on sixty years, first started when beer was tuppence a pint.' He studied the hard-packed Woodbine, ready for lighting. 'Aye, those were the days, a pennyworth of tobacco from that bar, and the clay pipe was free.' This remark solved the mystery of the various caches of used and broken clay pipes that I unearthed in the near vicinity of the pub during the years of my stay. Some were in quite good condition and I began a collection which included a few complete churchwardens. As the old man settled down to his second pint a large car pulled into the car park. Lunchtime trade, I thought excitedly as the couple entered the bar, this is what I must encourage, otherwise it's pure farce to open in the day and drink away the non-existent profit. Sylvia provided a generous spread of cold meats and pickles with various salad dressings and home-

baked finger rolls with local farm butter. They were obviously
enjoying the meal when the old villager re-opened his conversation with me.

'You haven't had that cesspit emptied, I hope, I dug it out
more than thirty years ago.' I began to feel decidedly uncomfortable; why on earth did he have to pick on that subject, I
thought as I glanced at my two diners. 'Aye,' he continued as
another Woodbine thumped the packet. 'I told the bloke who
had it before Bob Styles "Never take the lid off because as long
as it's sealed, little mites will live down there and eat it all."'

I caught the frown of my female customer as she finished
eating, to pat her lips with the serviette.

'Big thing that cesspit was in its day,' reminisced the old man
with a nostalgic tremor of emotion to his voice.

I wish you'd stay down there, thought the evil part of me as
my male customer ended his meal abruptly. I can ask him to
change the subject I thought, I really don't mind him going into
exile for another ten years, but how many other locals would I
lose in sympathy to him? He began to share his conversation
with the couple. 'Now we all got cesspits, but it was the bucket
before that, little stone buildings at the end of the garden with
mint growing one side and lavender the other, never a smell
with that growing there. Mine's a toolshed now.' His eyes
clouded as he searched his waistcoat pocket for the price of his
third pint. I hope you haven't got it, continued my evil thinking, but of all people the male customer offered to buy him a
drink which he accepted as a matter of course. 'Aye, those were
the days,' he continued after taking a liberal draught of the gift
but refusing their cigarette. 'Can't abide them fags with spats, I
like to taste the bacca I do. Aye, a bloke by the name of Nation
used to empty all our buckets in those days, had an old Ford
lorry with a tank on the back of it.' I made a futile interruption
about the weather, but he would not be silenced. 'Used to carry
'em on his shoulder he did, stink, you couldn't get near him
when he came in here for a pint, he'd end up on his own, and all
of us drinking outside.' The couple, despite the unsavoury

choice of subject, were enjoying his company and I realised that he was an essential part of village life that had vanished from many country pubs as they became 'modernised'.

Unfortunately progress had brought about the rape of the country inn; the growth of car-ownership made it accessible to the townspeople and the sanctuary of the villagers became invaded to the obvious delight of the innkeepers who had existed on a pittance for centuries.

The couple became regular customers from that day, calling weekly to meet the old man and hear his tales of the village, but they were an isolated case, and, despite all my effort and expense in providing a good spread of food, the morning trade remained abysmal. After enjoying the constant change and freedom of a salesman, I began to suffer the claustrophobic sensation of a prisoner within the ancient walls of the pub. I found myself envying the occasional representatives as their cars pulled away to another call, leaving me to my near solitary confinement and a nagging admission that I had done the wrong thing. But within a few weeks I was to pray for the return of my solitude when a stranger awaited my opening of the front door on a Monday morning.

He possessed a forceful personality with more than his share of the conversation and at first I accepted it as a pleasant change from my normal enforced silence, but he stayed for the whole morning. I closed the door behind him with the combination of a long bored yawn and a sigh of relief.

'There must be easier ways of earning a crust,' I joked to Sylvia later over a cup of tea. 'I've endured that blighter and his tongue for a solid four hours at a gross profit of one and threepence.' The following morning I stepped back in fearful surprise as he appeared once more on the stroke of opening time. 'Holidays?' I inquired, hoping that one or two weeks would be the sum total of my endurance.

'No, no,' he replied cheerfully between the loud clapping and rubbing of his hands. 'I've been put permanently on the night shift, suits me down to the ground, I do all my little odd jobs in the morning, then over here for a few hours before a late lunch, a good sleep and off to work again. I like this place,' he added. 'You can't hear yourself speak in those town pubs.'

'No you can't,' I agreed in utter depression as I pulled his pint and wishing it was a more potent drug than humble pale ale. As the weeks progressed I tried to ignore him, I whistled tunes as his voice droned on and on and on, I threw cases of empty bottles noisily around the cellar, and hit dry casks with my mallet, but he was invincible and shameless. 'What can I do about him?' I said to Sylvia after suffering his presence for a month. 'He's even discouraged the little casual trade I did enjoy, and any newcomers don't stay five minutes, he's just a continuous gramophone record, and patron saint of all pub bores.' We sat in deep thought as I continuously stirred my tea. 'The trouble is that I've no real reason to throw him out,' I continued. 'He holds his drink well, he's not a nuisance in the true sense of the word, he . . .'

'Freeze him out,' said Sylvia triumphantly. 'Don't light the fire, he won't last four hours in that temperature this time of the year. I'll borrow a couple of pairs of Dad's long underpants for you to wear. With some extra pullovers you'll survive while he shivers.'

The bore looked twice at my well-padded corpulent figure as I opened the door on the following Monday. More effort than usual went into his habitual hand clapping as he walked over to the lifeless fireplace.

'Coalman on strike then is he?'

'No,' I answered coldly. 'Can't afford a fire really, with trade such as this.'

The following morning he also appeared decidedly larger in a few more layers of protective clothing.

'That's it,' I later bellowed at Sylvia. 'I can take no more of him, it's like a morgue in there and he still keeps on with the vapour belching from his mouth like Scott of the Antarctic.' Later as I walked toward the pigsty with a half bucket of slops, Sylvia tapped the kitchen window.

'Why don't you try some of that on him?' she shouted through the glass with a wicked glint in her eyes. It took two days for the aversion treatment to take effect when he left the pub hurriedly after bravely consuming one pint, never to return again in my time. I later discovered that he was a well-known character who had outlived his welcome in all the pubs of the area, and I suppose that none were more pleased with his hurried departure than my boozy pigs.

'How did you survive the boredom of this miserable morning trade?' I asked my father-in-law during his daily call. 'It must have been purgatory for thirty years.' He nodded his agreement.

'Aye, many's the time I yearned for a good day's work instead of propping this bar up waiting for customers who never appeared. It wasn't till I encouraged the local gentry to use the place from time to time that it ever saw any trade in the morning.'

At that moment the council mobile library pulled into the car park. No horn blowing announced its arrival, only the throaty rumble of its diesel engine before the driver/librarian choked it into silence. He had scarcely taken his seat behind the small desk in the vehicle's doorway when as if from nowhere a dozen or more or the village bookworms appeared like magic for their weekly treat. I served the driver with a pint of ale and a ploughman's plate leaving him to enjoy the warmth of the new fire while I browsed for a book.

The library, I soon discovered, was also a meeting place, a gossip exchange, just like the converted bus that served as a mobile shop in the villages of the Vale. The conservative inhabitants rarely called in each other's homes like town dwellers. Their planned impromptu meetings invariably took place on board one of the convoy of service vehicles who supplied the village with its every need, and the drivers were the recognised channels of every item of information. News of a month-old pregnancy would be widespread by the slip of a tongue on board the county mobile clinic. But the most sought-after snippets of gossip always came from the lips of the travelling chemist who had a constant store of highly confidential gems for the eager ears of his customers.

All these invaluable characters called at the pub if only to pass the time of day as their customers browsed over the shelves. The nursing sister in charge of the clinic was most concerned over my health, and all other innkeepers for that matter. She was a very forthright person, obsessed with the health risks of smoking. I blushed like a guilty schoolboy as she entered the inn one lunchtime just as I was lighting a cigarette.

'Mr Brock,' she spat at me with her hands firmly placed on her hips, 'have you no respect for your family? Who will provide for them when you've smoked yourself into an early grave?'

Although I am now a non-smoker, the habit in those days was as common as eating, and the health hazard non-existent.

'Don't you realise', she continued, 'that publicans and bar staff are subjected to the same risk as heavy smokers even if they don't smoke?'

I obediently stubbed out my cigarette, inwardly dismissing her as a scare-mongering crank, but how true were her words when I recently saw a television programme on the same theme.

My father-in-law advised me to occupy the long-drawn morning hours with odd jobs within sight of the pub entrance, so I decided to give the building a new coat of white lime. My pending trouble was in the form of the ladder – it was too short. Despite my long reach the brush came within a tantalising foot and a half of the eave. The only risky solution involved placing it onto a builder's wheelbarrow to make up the elusive height. After securing the wheel with a wooden wedge on the slight incline of the car park, I gingerly began my ascent with a large bucket of white lime. My loaded brush was just about to apply the first coat beneath the black-pointed fascia board when I heard children's voices below. They were the two sons of an industrialist who lived on the perimeter of the village, normally well-behaved boys on leave from their boarding school, but, lacking the company of the local children who had returned a week earlier, they were bored and I was the chosen victim of their mischief. Suddenly, as I glanced down at their smiling faces, the ladder started to slide slowly down the wall, and involuntarily I began to paint a vertical white stripe as the wheelbarrow crept across the sloping car park. They met me when I stepped off the near horizontal ladder as if it had been a lift, with my bucket miraculously intact. Their blushing faces were at bursting point with suppressed laughter during my futile search for the missing wedge. I shielded my eyes from the early sun as they scanned the ridiculous line, and I realised the humorous spectacle I must have portrayed. With a fast action, I spun around to face them.

'Where's the wedge, you wicked little devils?' I screamed; but they were obviously ready for my onslaught when they quickly vacated the area.

I abandoned the wheelbarrow idea in favour of a longer ladder that I borrowed from the farm, but the old inn seemed to resent its facelift, for several times that I reached the eaves to begin painting a rare customer would appear, when I would hastily descend to discard my lime-speckled brown dust coat and revert to mine host with a white-spotted face.

The cellar was next to receive the treatment. The dank old walls had completely lost their identity of the mason's trowel marks through centuries of liming, and my mind travelled back in time trying to recreate a mental picture of the countless characters who had painted their layers on those old stones.

'You can make a start on my place when you've done that,' joked an old lady at the doorway. She was Mrs Evans from Higher End cottage, a quaint little figure holding her pension book after her weekly visit to the Post Office. She possessed a charming character and, despite their difference in age, she and Sylvia were staunch friends; but that was not uncommon in village life, where all age groups were compatible.

Some time later, and more as a selfish form of escapism, I left

Sylvia in charge of the pub while I re-decorated the interior of her cottage. She was thrilled beyond words as I pasted on the paper of her choice, and a week later her neat little home seemed to swell with pride over its first facelift in thirty years, but like all villagers she also had her pride, and the inevitable push-and-pull routine took place as she tried to force an envelope into my hand. I managed to deflect her persistence, but a few days later she arrived at the pub carrying a large cardboard box. Her face carried a very unusual feature of determination as she placed it on the counter.

'You must accept this please,' she said with an emotional tremor to her voice. 'I know how you and Sylvia love antiques, and this is the oldest thing I have next to the organ, but I don't suppose you want that old dust collector.' With that she was gone, and I opened the carton to reveal a fine Victorian oil lamp that we treasure greatly in memory of that sweet woman who was the essence of country charm.

That evening we had a darts match, a friendly with the neighbouring Green Dragon team. The result was secondary for the beer flowed freely and Sylvia's spread was eaten with gusto. At that time the breathalyser didn't exist and most people drank far in excess of its limit but one visitor named Sidney consumed enough for three men. His capacity was enormous and he showed little ill effect as he made for the doorway at closing time to be the last person out. I locked the bolts and set about my ritual of cleaning up, and tapping down the hard spiles in the casks to seal them off from their enemy, the air of the cellar. I listened subconsciously to the sound of Sidney's car as he started the engine, and the different tones as he went up through the gear box, but the noise remained static as the engine increased in speed. Suddenly there came a timid knock on the front door; when I opened it, there was Sidney.

'Something funny about the old car tonight,' he said with a slur to his voice. 'Or I've had a few too many. She went through the gears as sweet as a nut, and I'm sat there driving her as large as life, when I realised I haven't moved an inch.'

I glanced across the pub frontage to the faint outline of his car in the inky blackness of the night. 'Well there's not much we can do about it tonight,' I began in an effort to evade the situation. 'So I'll run you home and you can have a look at her tomorrow.'

He sat morosely by my side as we drove to his cottage, and it wasn't until the following day that I appreciated the strange sensation he had suffered, for the car had been jacked up onto concrete building blocks and its wheels stolen.

5 · Cuckoo Marans

M Y CATERING venture was an instant success, when by way of a gimmick I bought thirty Cuckoo Maran laying hens, large greyish birds who provided me with a daily basket of appetising dark brown eggs. These were placed on the counter near my limited menu of gammon steaks, beef steaks and mixed grills. The eggs did the trick: they presented an utterly irresistible farmhouse picture nestling in sweet fresh hay to tempt even the most blasé gourmet.

The profit margin left much to be desired, but the beer and general drink trade increased considerably to the delight of the brewery.

And then I made my first major and very costly blunder. I changed from kils to barrels. It is a rule of thumb that all average-gravity beers should be sold as soon as possible after tapping the cask, because like a bottle of wine it starts to die when opened to the air of the cellar. Three days should be the maximum; therefore a good cellarman should adjust his cask size to compare with his trade, which could range from a four and a half gallon firkin to a thirty-six gallon barrel. This I failed to do – the pub never in all its days warranted the introduction of barrels.

I began to hear stage whispers from disciples of my father-in-law. 'Must be the food,' was the general opinion. 'Beer and food don't mix, that's why you can never get a decent pint over the other place.' They were right to some extent, the arch enemy of beer being fat, and its worst form being potato crisps, which could turn a fine pint of beer into a very insipid drink when taken together. But my problem was over-capacity and the last thirty or forty pints had gone too old. I became reluctant to revert back to eighteen-gallon kils, believing my trade would warrant barrels in the coming summer months. But the summer came and went leaving a once gloriously happy band of pigs to lament the re-introduction of kils.

I soon redeemed my father-in-law's lost reputation, and once more the inn boasted the finest pint in the Vale. But I still believe firmly that the drinking public are rather gullible.

I was busy engaged cooking meals in my little kitchen next to the lounge bar one hectic Saturday evening when the barmaid popped her head in. 'Home Brew's off,' she said.

Leaving my steaks to fend for themselves, I rushed to the cellar, and changed over to a new cask. But I suffered the penalty of wearing too many hats. A chef and a cellarman are not compatible. My once succulent grills were cremated to little black crusts. They had been sacrificed so that the beer might flow. Near to closing time when the meals had finished I took off my whites to revert to mine host. The appraisal of the beer in the lounge bar was abnormally high, with the accolade of 'Bob Styles will never die while you're around.' As I cleaned the cellar the following morning with my ego still pulsating, my eyes followed the solitary plastic pipe snaking from the lounge bar. It was connected to a kil of pale ale, the cheapest 'boys' beer' or 'cooking ale' as the regulars named it. In all innocence I had more than satisfied a bar full of grateful customers with a kil of inferior beer, and made a handsome profit in doing so.

But it's not only beer that can sometimes fool the consumer; many ardent whisky drinkers can never tell a brand if put to the test. One particular incident involving my infamous father-in-law proves my point. A few year prior to my taking over I called at the Six Bells one lunchtime. It was empty, and Bob was busy cleaning his shotguns in the cellar. Suddenly a large black Daimler saloon swerved into the car park.

'Oh, my God,' he said, hastily cleaning his hands of the gun oil. 'It's Mr Mayne and his party, I haven't got any of their brand. They won't stay.' He browsed along a shelf containing empty whisky bottles of every conceivable brand, and their purpose was about to be revealed to me. 'That's the one,' he said, taking a famous shaped bottled from the collection. 'Now we'll fill him up with this one, and they'll never know the difference.'

The five middle-aged men entered the bar – Cardiff business types on one of their occasional excursions to the country. Mr Mayne eyed the small selection of optics and his expression beamed into satisfaction.

'Ah, you have it, Robert, no self-respecting publican would be without it. We'll start with a glass each of your best bitter and five doubles of the staff of life.'

I had to look away as they sipped their potions; fear of exposure was more than bearable. My father-in-law looked on without the slightest feature of deceit as they savoured the fiery liquid and proclaimed the merits of the fake brand. The ultimate deception was yet to come when Robert had to refill the famous bottle with yet another different brand. At closing time three totally different bottles of whisky, under the guise of their choice, had been consumed, and the party left in high spirits, full of praise for a publican who knew what whisky to stock.

I later discovered that even a habitual brandy drinker can be duped. He was a young chap, just under thirty, I would say, with an enormous capacity for alcohol. His evening would start with three or four pints of Home Brew ale, before changing to his favourite tipple, a famous French three-star brandy. On the night in question, his friend had pre-arranged with me to change the brand, while using the same bottle. I stood to win a pound if the deception was not proven. The only substitute, however, was a cheap bottle of coarse South African grape brandy, so the label stated. It had been in the cellar for years, no doubt waiting for someone to have the audacity to put it in the optic. Our victim consumed it with relish, I collected my wager and the episode ended in a good laugh all round, but in the years that followed, especially through the breathalyser slump, I must confess that the options of fraud were very tempting to make ends meet.

Our first Christmas arrived to allow us the one night off in the year. How we enjoyed that half-day. Sylvia sighed as we played with our two children. 'At least they have each other's company,' she said. 'I was a real loner, often wondered if I had any parents.' I realised then her reluctance to return to the life she grew up in and the solitude she abhorred.

During January of the new year, a new county type arrived at one of the morning sessions, a middle-aged, tweed-dressed man with an expensive purple nose and a deep red face to match. He came right to the point with me after making his acquaintance to the company. 'Young Brock, my keeper tells me he needs six hundred pheasant poults this year, how many can you provide?'

Pheasant rearing was another of my father-in-law's sidelines, which I assumed had retired with him, but it was not to be. I could do it, but it was so time-consuming. My mind raced for an excuse, but he was an extremely dominant character, and a close friend of the brewery directors.

I did some calculations, the Cuckoo Marans would soon be broody, and they could cover twenty eggs each. If half my number decided to be maternal, that would be three hundred poults to hatch.

'Damn it, thought you'd do the lot, old boy,' he snorted briskly. 'Never mind, that's half the bounders.' He continued with a raucous laugh, 'Have to send the old girl to bed, she can cover the rest.'

This was all part of my father-in-law's inheritance, a gamekeeper, a farmer and to some extent a publican. This is what he had groomed me for. No complete stranger could ever take it on, and he could never see it die in his time, even if I might. The smallholding comprised six beef cattle, one milking cow for calf rearing, three sows and litters, about sixty chickens, two goats, rabbits, ferrets and the annual pheasant-rearing routine. Thankfully, the quarter of an acre of vegetable garden had been converted into a car park. It was little wonder that my father-in-law had retired with heart trouble.

I also had the additional role of chef, and I could have dispensed with the smallholding, but it was such a pleasant sanctuary from the demanding attention of the pub, a form of safety valve. The late spring weeks began to build up to the crescendo of summer activity, not to mention the migration of fifty of my hard-earned pheasant poults.

It was before the days of cordless telephones, and my baby-crying alarm buzzed from the bar just as I was putting the food into one of the rearing pens. 'The bitter's off,' squeaked the tinny voice of the barmaid. It was always an urgent duty, no one likes to wait for their drinks. As I headed towards the pub a loud flutter of wings caused me to look back. It was a beautiful sight, but expensive for me, as fifty young pheasants flew in the direction of the estate of our squire. I later informed his gamekeeper who was elated and rewarded me with a pint for my trouble.

During the peak of the summer season a young Frenchman

approached me in my kitchen, I recognised him as the propri-
etor of a top Cardiff restaurant. At first I felt rather humble in
his presence as I prepared my meals, then I consoled myself as
he admired my splendid deep brown Cuckoo Maran eggs with
true Gallic enthusiasm. He had a proposition that I sub-let him
an area of the pub for conversion to a restaurant at his cost.
The obvious place would be upstairs where two large rooms
had gathered dust for at least thirty years. I enjoyed them as
they were. They had a dry fusty smell that I could relate to a
Dickens story. The children loved to play there, and Sylvia
could often be found retracing her childhood amidst the piles
of junk. She was far from enthusiastic over the Frenchman's
proposal and I detected a spirit of tradition in her attitude. My
rejection of the offer was made easy when I realised that I
would receive no part of the restaurant's drink trade, and so
the two old rooms had a reprieve for our children's adventures
and Sylvia's daydreams.

As the autumn came, so the fruitful Vale of Glamorgan
began to yield its produce. The grass crops had been made as
hay and silage, now it was the turn of the harvest grains as
combines purred away from dawn to dusk.

At times the Six Bells' car park resembled a farmyard when
thirsty workers stopped by, and their tractors outnumbered
cars. These were idyllic days for country people when the
balmy air trembled with activity. All too soon hibernation
would follow.

But farming has much sadness in relation to the animal
world. So-called pests such as pigeons and grey squirrels must
be controlled for crop survival and, when you think of it, rarely
does livestock die of natural causes. They are slaughtered to
feed the insatiable appetites of an ever-increasing population.
Intensive farming is frowned upon by many, yet old-fashioned
methods would never accommodate the enormous demands of
today. The battery hen is the food martyr of modern times, a
pathetic egg machine, who must welcome death – but even
they are survivors, for I know one who escaped.

The large multi-cage lorry from the poultry-processing factory had called at the local egg farmer for its quota of off-peak layers. Not for them a half-dozen warm summers laying their natural eggs on free range. They were not profitable below a sixty per cent production level. Their next payment to the human race is meat. The driver finished his drink and the throaty diesel pulled away from the car park. As I dried my glasses and browsed through the daily newspaper spread on the counter, I was aware of the cluck, cluck of a hen. Even by battery standards she must have rated the most miserable specimen of all time. Practically featherless, with savage wounds of cannibalism inflicted by her other inmates, she picked her way cautiously into the pub entrance.

That one deserves to live, I thought, as I called for my daughter, Susan. She looked at it in disbelief after the obvious mental comparison of our own fine hens.

'What are we going to do with it?' she said with a child's frown.

'We can't keep her with the Marans,' I answered, 'they'll finish her off. Put her in one of the pheasant pens, let her see grass for the first time in her life.'

By the spring, the transformation was unbelievable. She was a fine brown majestic hen, who strutted her domain with dignity and rewarded us with an egg a day. Natural living allowed her to become broody by early summer, and Susan placed three goose eggs from the farm in her nest. Only one fine gander hatched out, a devoted son who protected her with all the ferocity of his kind. But we concealed our little story in fear of offending the egg farmer who struggled hard to make a living even with his controversial intensive methods.

I was often told during my training course that a good publican follows the pattern of the famous three little monkeys portrait. 'Hear all, see all and say nowt.' Nowhere more than a country pub was this edict so necessary. It was obviously prudent as an example to ignore the ugly facets of modern factory farming with tongue in cheek over the stressful living conditions of these unfortunate animals. My emotional feelings of the hunt were suppressed while no allegiance was offered to their arch-enemies, the saboteurs. The ever-explosive subject of politics was always evaded like a deadly nightshade when a left-wing farm labourer could be criticising the capitalist system in earshot of a Tory landowner just the other side of the beer pumps. I sometimes wondered if I might be in danger of losing my identity and character by remaining mute on matters that were so close to my heart, but as the months progressed I learned that the ringing tone of the cash register was much more important than my principles.

6 · The Blizzard

THE SIX BELLS provided an above-average quota of characters who unwittingly swelled the revenue of the pub by virtue of their audiences. Perhaps I could blame their long-standing familiarity, but it wasn't until our second winter that I realised their true value. It was Boxing Day as I opened the door for the morning session to an experience never witnessed before in the village. A flock of Arctic geese in V-formation flew in low and noisily from the north. Dai Jones, the oldest male inhabitant, shielded his eyes to look up as he paused in the front car park. It smacks of an Irish joke, but as he neared his eighties, he found it easier on his lungs to negotiate the steep Baron Hill backwards.

'Didn't know Price Moulton kept that many birds,' he said with a mischievous smile and panting breath. The flock were clearly heading for the hamlet of Moulton where farmer Price did keep a few geese, but his were certainly not airborne types.

I pointed at the formation as it grew smaller against the backing of an ominous grey sky. 'They're from Russia, Dai, too cold for them up there, they have to come south.' The radio had recently supplied me with this gem of information but Dai gave me all the credit as he made for the bar fire. 'Fairplay, you're a long-headed bugger you are.' It also earned him a free pint that I gave to the few senior citizens from time to time, but it was Boxing Day when the tradition was a free drink for every regular. The till suffered as rather more than the usual amount of locals rallied for my Yuletide gift; by midday the two bars pulsed with activity as a constant flow of urban people passed on their way to the annual meet of the Glamorgan Hunt at Cowbridge Common.

Despite the controversy of field sporting activities, of which I am reasonably open-minded, the Christmas card scene is a rural institution of this country. It's only a pity that wildlife has to suffer in the name of 'sport', not that the sportsmen ever catch that many.

With the exception of funerals it was rare to see the Bells so busy during the morning session, and it wasn't uncommon to close the door at three-thirty without having seen a customer. The four hours could linger on like eternity, while the occupational temptation of over-indulgence through sheer boredom posed a constant threat. In actual fact we obtained reasonable takings only for the final two and a half hours of most evenings, a vivid contrast to a busy town pub where the till rings non-stop from opening to closing time. But the Bells, like many of the Vale of Glamorgan inns, was never a great money-spinner in those days. It was a cottage tenancy where innkeeping took third place to the licensee holding a job elsewhere and augmenting his income with the proceeds of the smallholding.

When my father-in-law took it on in the early 1930s the cost of the ingoing inventory was £12 for wet stock and glasses. His predecessor was a strong character, a Somerset man with the nickname of Bridgwater Bob. It was long before the days of the treble chance fortunes that a modest pools win enabled him to realise a life-long dream of being a publican. He and his son enjoyed their cups to the extent of neglecting the agricultural side of the business, but Bob, ever a raconteur, discovered that the village needed a wet fish supplier. I was indebted to old Dai Jones for these gems of the pub's history. He had a habit of keeping his thumbs behind his trousers' braces as he reminisced.

'Couldn't face a pint here on a Friday. Bob would come up from the kitchen stinking of fish with scales all over his hands and he had a habit of holding the pint by the handle with his blasted thumb inside the pot.' Bill Probert, the unofficial mayor of the village by virtue of his self-taught intellect, often quoted the final days of Bridgwater Bob.

'I remember it well,' he would say to an eager audience of townspeople as he donned his wood and string chain of office made by a local wag. 'Strolls up for my pint about eight o'clock, and it's all shut, just a chink of light from the cellar window shutter. "Come on Bob," I shouts. "Let's have you – I'm dying for a pint" and do you know what he shouts back? "Not tonight, Bill, I'm sorry but there's only enough beer here for me and the boy." ' It appears that the fish business failed to subsidise the cost of father and son's insatiable thirst and they returned to a more sober life in the nearby town of Barry.

The maturing characters of my time were Ray Vizard and Shirty Thomas. Raymond, as he liked to be addressed, was a stonemason and jobbing builder employing his cousin Shirty as a labourer, who insisted he was destined for a higher station in life. Raymond entered the bar to shrug his shoulders with a shiver. He had what I term a bumble bee voice and he always opened his conversation with 'Aye, it's bloody cold, boss, I think I'll 'ave a drop of firewater to start, make it a double. Did you see them ducks go over this morning? That's a sign of bad weather.'

Shirty followed close behind. 'Not ducks, Raymond.'

'Well, what the 'ell do you reckon they were, eagles?'

Shirty possessed a matter-of-fact attitude that any theory he offered was correct and final. 'Puffins, Raymond, puffins from Lundy Island, too cold out there, they're coming inland for warmth.' He took a liberal draught from his pint leaving a line of white froth on his dark moustache as he looked along the bar for any sign of dissent.

Raymond looked up at the ceiling in contempt. 'Why the 'ell don't you leave the bird-watching to ornithologists, or whatever they calls 'em, Shirty?'

And so it would go on, like two stand-up comics, for hour after hour. Shirty with his theories, Raymond with his caustic cynicism, yet they would never hear a bad word against each other, and that was the theme of all the genuine villagers, for the majority were related. Their families were large – one could boast a complete football team – and their cottages were small, where four children to a bed was not unusual.

I caught the eye of old Mrs Reagan at the front door as she timidly held her quart china jug. Her husband Danny was terminally ill, but for two years she carried out her daily errand of mercy to provide him with his beloved pint. He was a wonderful character of original Irish stock who was always given the freedom of the pub on St Patrick's Day. 'If bread's the staff of life,' he would say after a rendition of 'Danny Boy', 'then the Bells' beer must be the liquid of life.'

These people were the backbone of the pub, they did little to swell the coffers – beer drinkers never do – but the Bells was theirs, they created the atmosphere, without them it would be like a motorway café for people on their way through. I often wondered what rivalry existed when the village had three pubs, but the Red Cow and the Rose and Crown had long since been private dwellings, leaving the Six Bells in splendid isolation.

That afternoon as the temperature dropped I stoked the two bar fires and 'bottled up' for the evening session. Down at the holding I laid new straw for the pig beds, and envied them as they nestled down for the night. The Cuckoo Marans had called it a day as they argued with each other for perch places in the warmth of the henhouse. Bessie, the old Jersey milking cow, gave me a long maternal stare with her irresistible brown eyes. I had dispensed with cattle rearing, but I felt honour-bound to buy in a spring calf to savour her natural instincts. She seemed to read my intentions as she chewed on the sweet-smelling hay of her manger. I gave a sigh and chuckled to myself, it was all so hopelessly natural. The Marans were not laying, it was too cold and the days were too short. The pigs were too light because they free-ranged and the cow was nearly dry. I cursed my thoughts. How on earth would the country survive on methods such as mine; it had to be intensive despite the cruelty for the sake of survival. I subconsciously cracked the ice of the various drinking troughs, they wouldn't be used any more that night, and the morning would see them just as solid. My human drinkers will not allow their drinks to freeze, I thought, as I made for the pub.

It was strange, but for the first time I noticed a ridge-shaped fillet of cement on the chimney breast. It was a foot higher than the slate roof. The thatching line I realised. What stories you could tell, I thought, you creak and squeak and bump in the night and you're supposed to have a ghost, but you're so secretive. The evening of Boxing Day was quieter than expected, and the club atmosphere of the local villagers prevailed. The topic was the wartime Penmark Home Guard. It was uncanny, but I noticed that they would reminisce only when there were no outsiders, or very few, within earshot. They were the first to confess that their contribution to the war effort was doubtful.

'Bloody uniforms and boots were handy for work,' said one.

'Aye, but didn't we look a mess at the church parades in Barry,' said another. 'I remember Dai Jones turning up in wellies for one big do, royalty it was. He'd worn his boots out at the cement works.'

My father-in-law joined in. 'I wish they'd have given us shotguns instead of those Enfield rifles though, hell of a job to hit a rabbit an' if you did hit one, you blew him to bits.'

Another local entered, a rather brusque fellow who had the habit of counting the exact coinage for his drink, before crashing it down onto the counter with all his might. 'Pint of best bitter, landlord,' was his high-pitched command after reducing Dad's Army to complete silence. Now one of the many practices that I inherited from my father-in-law was the storage of glasses and tankards 'right side up'. He once told me, 'If you place a hot slightly damp glass on the shelf upside down it will trap stale air and affect the beer.' I thought it an old wives' tale, but I followed tradition as I produced the coin-banger's glass tankard from beneath the counter right side up. Part of the expertise of pint pulling is that bar staff rarely look at the glass as they fill it. The beer engine lifts a half pint per pull. As I placed the pint on the counter after two pulls, a huge black spider began to emerge from the bubbling froth like a scene from a horror film. I have a high regard for spiders and felt sorry for that poor fellow, who in the middle of his slumber beneath the counter had been blasted into an enforced binge. But my customer was not amused as his face whitened.

'What's that thing doing there,' he screamed. As quick as a flash the inimitable Shirty Thomas supplied the answer as he rushed over with an air of superior knowledge to inspect the creature.

'Any pub worth its salt got to keep a few of those around,' he said as he rubbed his index finger along his moustache. 'Beer flies, the place would be overrun with the buggers if it weren't for the likes of him there in your pint.'

As I emptied the glass with the inebriated spider into the slop bucket I queried the wisdom of my father-in-law's theory, for a building as old as the Six Bells would always house its fair quota of spiders.

Sadly, closing time came around all too fast, and I stood by the front door after my last customer had left. My breathing was ominously visible in spurts of steaming white vapour, and as I took in the utter silence of the village, small flurries of powdery snow crossed the arc of the single street light. A cow in the field opposite coughed and with a smug selfish attitude I felt that my stock were under cover, warm and safe from the threatening storm, as I climbed the stairs to bed. I lay in bed the following morning, reluctant to leave the mound of blankets so essential to a pub as cold as the Bells. The silence of the village was even more intense. Ice was formed on the inside of the windows as I peered through the obscure glass. In close pursuit of the Arctic geese the snow had arrived, not a token blanket, but in drifts as high as doorways. I experienced a surge of childhood excitement as I raced to dress, leaving Sylvia to her deep slumber. A few hours later my enthusiasm had turned to frustration as I fought to dig a passage from the pub door to the road. Luckily, the rear car park, like most of the surrounding fields, had been kept reasonably clear of snow by the high winds, and I was able to reach the stock with little difficulty.

It must have been a unanimous thought for all the villagers to meet at the pub, for I soon had a bar full of people, including villagers who didn't drink. We were cut off, there was little doubt about that. The mile and a quarter long lane up to the main road was 'Blocked with a continuous six foot drift,' said Bill, the local farmer, in his philosophical manner. These are a wonderful breed of people, constantly matching themselves against the elements for what must be a labour of love. Financially their assets are enormous, quite often exceeding a quarter of a million pounds, yet their income bears no relationship to such a massive investment; in fact they work around the clock for a lower wage then the average manual worker.

Bill winked at some villagers across the bar as a party of people began to formulate a plan of action. They were classed as 'townie newcomers' despite a residence of more than ten years in some cases.

'How's the beer looking, Derek?' shouted Ray Vizard from the rear of the bar. 'As long as that lasts out I can take a winter of this just like they do in Canada.'

The contingency preparations went on despite the constant sarcasm of the villagers, who had obviously weathered several blizzards, but none so ferocious as that one. Two tractors and a Land-Rover were brought into use, but they were no match for the endless wall of snow that filled our service road. The only way to reach civilisation was by way of the fields to the end of Cardiff Airport runway, then onto the main road and the large village of Rhoose, which had a good selection of shops. Each day the 'Patrol', as they were nicknamed by the reluctant villagers, called on the houses of the elderly people to list their requirements. The situation was never dire enough to warrant the necessity of their journey, more so to recapture their youthful spirit of adventure. While my old Bessie and the Marans did little to supplement the food shortage, the local farm was more than capable of supplying the basic needs. On the third day Shirty watched through the pub window as they started on their daily journey, each man pulling his hastily improvised sledge.

'There goes Scott of the Antarctic and his gang,' he laughed, but the day was not far distant before he would eat humble pie. The beer was fast running out, and while Shirty was prepared to starve, thirst would never be the cause of his death.

It was most certainly an ill wind that brought me some good by way of the blizzard, but with the last day of the old year just two days away I had visions of it being a dry one at that current rate of consumption. I coupled up the last eighteen-gallon kil of Pale Ale and crossed my fingers that the dray would arrive soon; but that dream was futile. The road was still well and truly blocked, while our pleas to the highway department fell on deaf ears for they had more important roads to clear. I had not seen my father-in-law for nearly a week, but he kept in touch by phone. In one way I missed him, but it was a relief to be free of his constant yet unintentional supervision. Shirty was the first customer that evening and also the recipient of a pint from the new cask. His face winced as if sucking a lemon when he took his first large drink. He was normally an inn-keeper's dream with rarely a complaint.

'That's a bit on the sharp side, Derek.' I took a sip from his pot; it was like vinegar. I rushed to the phone to consult my mentor for no course had trained me for that fault.

'Take out the spile and have a smell,' said Bob Styles. 'Sounds like a "Stinker" cask, nothing you can do about it if it is.'

I rushed back to the cellar. He was right, it was an odour similar to propane gas. I kicked the cask in temper whilst voicing my scorn for Shirty to hear.

'Well, that's bloody well that, now what are you going to do?' I drew him into the problem, as if he was to blame, when the true culprit was the cask 'sniffer' at the brewery. I often thought that my father-in-law was pulling my leg when he spoke of a man whose daily routine was to smell the inside of casks, but one of the risks of a wooden barrel is the rare inconsistency of the material from which it is manufactured, Russian Oak. Generations of coopers have chosen Memel timber to fashion the staves of their cask, but periodically the mighty tree will produce absorbent rogue wood, and one such bolshie had decided to be the last cask in my cellar.

'The blasted sniffer must have been drunk,' I shouted at Shirty with the emotional tremor of a legionnaire who had lost his water flask. An air of pessimism prevailed in the bar that night as my bottled beer stock began to diminish. They were mainly hardened draught drinkers, devout religious fanatics of Hancock's Pale Ale, and the gassy substitute merely created expressions of internal wind on their dejected faces. Nearly closing time Shirty approached me.

'Derek, we've worked out a plan of action, we hate to admit it, but we got to do the same as the townies. If you can get the brewery to deliver a couple of casks to the airport buffet bar, me and Raymond will knock up a couple of sledges.'

'They'll be far heavier than groceries,' I answered.

He replied with his usual deep chuckle, 'You leave the husky side of it to us. We'll pull it from the brewery in Cardiff if we have to.'

Our luck held the following day. The dray was making a delivery to the Rhoose Social Club, and the brewery agreed to leave two kils at the airport. I couldn't miss the adventure, and even more so when Shirty arrived at the pub. His Arctic survival clothing, as he called it, consisted of metallic grey fertiliser bags from the farm. He wore one on each leg tied at the thighs with hay cord, plus another like a jerkin with cut arm holes.

Tears streamed down Ray Vizard's face as he taunted him. 'You look like a clapped-out bloody Martian, Shirty.'

His reply was instantaneous. 'Well I'm not kidding, Raymond, but this is what they told the SAS to do when they dropped 'em in Norway during the war if ever they lost their protective clothing.'

I doubt that plastic bags existed at that time, but no one risked the futility of disputing him.

The outward journey was delightful as our party of eight covered the distance like schoolboys when we played, wrestled and threw snowballs. The wildlife tracks over the virgin snow was a pleasant reminder of the normally shy activities of the country creatures, and a feeling of well-being existed as we arrived at the Rhoose Social Club for refreshment. Two hours later in very high spirits, after informing air traffic control that two kils of beer would be using their northern runway, we set off like a party of Klondyke prospectors.

The homeward journey was not so idyllic. Despite the cajoling of Shirty with his cries of 'Mush, mush' the heavy casks constantly became bogged down in patches of deep snow, sometimes vanishing completely into ditches, as we negotiated hedgerows. I had serious doubts that it would settle by the New Year, and the possibility crossed my mind that it would never be drinkable again after such an eventful journey. We

suddenly confronted the townies as they entered the large
swede field near the village perimeter. They were outward-
bound on an afternoon foray. The friendly sarcasm from both
sides developed into a furious snowball battle only to termin-
ate when all contestants realised that ours was an errand of
mercy.

Unlike the fickle higher-gravity Home Brew the PA settled in
record time, and I began to serve it later that evening, but I had
the distinct feeling of trying to satisfy the thirst of the multitude
on a mere thirty-six gallons. Shirty was also aware of the
situation, and positioned himself at the end of the counter to
control over-zealous imbibers of the precious ale. One thing
was certain, no outsiders would call to share our rations. The
village was utterly cocooned and muffled in a massive white
blanket. A bulldozer had started to clear our service road over
a mile away. Its progress was painfully slow due to the nature
of the job in which the snow could not be pushed aside, but
removed to wider roadside verges by lorries. There was little

fear of the police calling on me after closing time, and I was somewhat relaxed from my usual fear of the extremely precise ten-forty call of the inspector and sergeant from Barry. The Penmark police station had long since closed, but without any pressure on my part the regulars left on time. There was a moral somewhere in their minds that an angel could lead them, but the devil would never drive them. The morning of the last day of the old year dawned, and I was happy in the fact that I had one complete kil of Pale Ale, as well as various bottled beers, and plenty of wine and spirits to take us into the New Year, and to blazes with the future.

My daughter Susan, who had been enjoying a glorious time throughout the emergency with all the other village children, rushed into the bar near the end of the morning session.

'Dad, Dad,' she gasped in a breathless abundance of child-hood energy. 'There's winter sports down the Church Field. It's really marvellous, Dad, you must come, please.'

Curiosity got the better of me as I locked up and headed for the steep field on the south side of the village. The complete village population must have turned out for the affair including old Annie Thomas who was nearly a hundred. Conveyances of all shapes and sizes from expensive toboggans to metal tin trays hurtled down the Cwm run as it had been christened. Further along on more virgin snow a few of the townies made an attractive picture in their continental ski outfits, but the star of the show was Shirty on a sheet of corrugated iron. He had bent back the front to slightly resemble a bobsleigh and with a running push from Ray Vizard, who jumped on as the contraption gained momentum, they sped toward the Cwm at breakneck speed to land in the icy water of the brook.

That evening will always be a jewel in my memory, it was just like a big village party with no fear of intrusion, and I am sure there were many of us who wished the snow was a permanent winter feature. But our dreams of a Swiss isolated splendour within the Vale of Glamorgan were far from practical without a source of revenue. By one-thirty we were in bed beneath the sheer pressure of the blanket mound when I thought I heard the bark of a diesel engine.

Sylvia with her acute sense of hearing sat upright. 'Can't be the farm this time of night, listen, there it is again.'

I rushed to the window as the village suddenly emerged from its slumber. Bedroom lights switched on and front doors opened as the bulldozer entered the village like a lonely monster. Its powerful spotlights pierced the darkness of the road to reveal excited groups of inhabitants. The siege was over. I invited the weary-eyed driver to a well-earned drink and he was eagerly followed by Shirty and a dozen regulars. I sensed a feeling of sadness as we reminisced, that it was all over; tomorrow our little Shangri-la would be invaded by the outside world, but the brewery dray would receive many hands of welcome to the pub with no beer.

7 · The Fox

THE BLIZZARD left its mark with isolated patches of hard-packed snow right to the beginning of spring when the sheer magic of that exciting season permeated the Vale. Little wonder it is named the 'Garden of Wales', this long, rolling, productive valley as it runs parallel to the Bristol Channel between Cardiff and Bridgend. Its hamlets, villages and farms are endless, each community centred on a church and pub, and sometimes a general store with a sub-post office. Someone is at home in most dwellings yet an uncanny silence prevails when the proverbial pin could be heard to drop, a silence broken only by animal or farm machinery sounds.

My own silence was interrupted each morning only by the welcome greeting of our elderly vicar as he walked his lonely daily pilgrimage to an empty church. He was an extremely articulate person, having been a soldier in the First World War, and later an Oxford Fellow. We often discussed life seated on barrels in the cellar when I would query the futility of his weekday service.

His answer was always the same as he braved all weathers, even the blizzard, to provide the service of God. 'Wouldn't it be a sin if someone turned up and I wasn't there.'

We often referred to the period of my marriage, how he insisted on baptising me before carrying out the service. I later discovered through my elder sister that I had been christened as a baby, and when I told him his humour prevailed with 'Just as well, perhaps it didn't take the first time.'

He persuaded me to take up bell-ringing, but, to use a pun, I never quite got the hang of it – the bell rope usually rang me. My patience came to an end during practice one evening when the local thatcher arrived late. He rushed up the belfry steps leaving the trap door open just at my rear, and I stepped back into a rapid descent to dislocate my shoulder. This mishap became a hardy annual at future campanologist suppers over the Six Bells, when the vicar would always include it as a humorous anecdote within his speech.

Marriages and funerals could provide the pub with excellent revenue, the latter taking preference over weddings. It is an ill wind that blows good and my record lunch-time sale of two kils was due to a very popular chap who now rests in peace at the churchyard. The other people to share my cellar for world-wide discussion were the draymen, wonderful men whom I envied for their total immunity to the effects of alcohol. Also, despite an excellent sense of decorum, they provided an information service on neighbouring pubs. I don't know how they would survive in these days of the breathalyser, but twelve to twenty pints a working day was quite an average consumption. My father-in-law often re-enacted the scene of his first day as a second drayman at Hancock's Brewery.

'A Sentinel steam lorry we had,' he would say. 'She was loaded ready to go with full pressure when my mate, Jack Stokes, walks across from the order office seriously studying the delivery list. "Eighteen calls we got, lad," he says. "There's a pint in all of 'em except that mingy sod, and he won't give you a drop off his nose, so we'll 'ave to buy one there." '

They are strong men and I believe the secret of their sobriety lies in their heavy labour, for they have little respect for drunkenness, but an admiration for feats of strength. Work hard and drink hard was their motto with a beer-sampling ability second to none. Bob Styles must obviously be their patron saint for he possessed more than his share of these essential qualities, and to this day younger draymen who never personally knew him speak in reverential terms whenever they discuss him.

The spring, unfortunately, brought the poachers to the countryside. For some I have respect, as they go about their unlawful business in a humane manner, but the majority of these trigger-happy hooligans I abhor. They will shoot anything that moves regardless of season, age or sex. Three such characters in a battered van screeched to a halt in the car park as I had just completed my cleaning routine one morning. The chore was yet another inheritance from Bob Styles but was worthwhile to see the pub so obviously cared for. Customers they may have been, but how I despised them. In boots moulded with heavy clay soil they oafishly despoiled my polished floor, and carpet square. Bob Styles would have ordered them out in no mean terms to clean their footwear, but I lacked the courage. I cursed inwardly for their miserable profit of three-pence per pint when they expected a holy right to defile two hours of hard work. They possess an intellect for the spit and sawdust bars of the large urban brewery-managed houses where beer consumption is the main criterion at any cost, with cleaners employed to follow them. But I was a self-employed tenant, paying rent to the brewery for my home. Why should I tolerate those people, I thought, as they spoilt the hard-won lustre of my brass and copperware? But I held my tongue as their conversation centred on the morning's sport.

'Got more money than sense, he 'ave,' said one, 'blasting that partridge and her chicks, must 'ave got through five rounds.'

'Ah, lay off, will you?' replied the culprit, whom I immediately began to hate. 'Bloody good fun it was, they scattered everywhere after I killed the mother. The little buggers took some killing, I'll tell you.'

Shaking with temper, I quietly made for the public phone in the hall. It was our only phone and I spoke in little more than a whisper to the Rhoose police station. It was a small office, sometimes unmanned, but thankfully the constable I wished to speak to answered. He was a hunting, shooting and fishing person who lived strictly by the sporting rule-book. I didn't relish my informer's role, but these were a thoroughly nasty trio, and although I reared pheasants to be hunted, I felt their act of carnage was despicable. The police van arrived within twenty minutes, and through the corner of my eye I saw the constable peer into the rear of their vehicle. He removed his helmet as he entered the bar, while expressions of surprise and guilt crossed their faces.

His questions were quick and to the point. 'Is that your van in the car park, gentlemen?' They nodded. 'Do you have permits for the shotguns?' They were obviously well seasoned to police interrogations, answering only with a nod or shake of the head. The constable commandeered their weapons, saying they could be retrieved on production of the relevant permits at Rhoose police station. He told me many months later that they never appeared, and I felt that some form of debt, however futile, had been settled with the unfortunate partridge and her chicks.

I earnestly wanted to dispense with pheasant rearing; it was a rewarding and enjoyable pastime, but time-consuming during my busy period. To prepare the nests, which were the old-fashioned double-section wooden orange boxes, I had to dig a good-sized grassy turf for the base which held the moisture to stop the eggs from becoming brittle. On top of the turf I would put a good layer of meadow hay, and then the eggs, between fifteen and twenty, depending on the size of the hen. Mr Mortimer, from a neighbouring village, provided the sittings, but the scarcity of broody hens was a growing problem of modern times. Virtually extinct are the maternal old breeds such as Rhode Island Reds, Buff Orpingtons and my own Cuckoo Marans. In their place scientists have created a hybrid battery hen whose sole purpose in life is to lay as many eggs in the shortest time without her natural instinct of going broody. So acute was the problem to pheasant rearers that I was constantly wooed by gamekeepers to loan or sell them my coveted Marans. Even Sylvia's uncle, the head keeper to Sir David Evans' Bevan Estate at Margam, travelled the round journey of eighty miles to plead with me for the celebrated Marans. Naturally, I should have searched for a Maran cockerel, and the future of their breed would have been secure in the Vale at least. It was as I was tending to my sitting hens one day that someone approached me with that idea in mind. He was obvious county type by his style of dress, which seems to be their standard uniform: green wellingtons, fawn cavalry twill trousers, navy blue crew-neck pullover topped with an expensive peak cap. He had established an area of his estate to conserve the original species of our heritage before they became extinct. He had a Maran cockerel eagerly awaiting a courtship, so I could hardly refuse him the sale of two of my precious birds to preserve their superb breed.

With the spring came another seasonal chore to coincide with my busy period. The rear of the pub was surrounded by a bank of hedgerow which required constant attention to keep the growth in trim. It was similar to the Forth Bridge painting job. As I completed the circuit, so the start of my labours had grown again. Yet it was all good therapy for a licensee whose normal existence would only be within the confines of a smoke-laden bar. Little wonder that insurance companies loaded their life premiums for the profession. Thankfully I could afford the luxury of a barmaid during the summer months to relieve me from the morning session, as Sylvia was still very much committed to our son Stewart, who was just over two. He kept on my tail most of the time, but he required quite a back-up service on her part. Our daughter Susan, who was nine, appeared for meals only between spending an idyllic childhood with her friends in the fields and woodland surrounding the village. Sylvia had grown up in the same environment and accepted our way of life with a positive attitude, yet, like all country children, she admitted that the attractions of urban life beckoned her strongly once she had reached her teens.

The pheasants had hatched, and were just a week old when I decided to release the Marans and their broods from their confined rearing pens into the large wire-covered pheasantry. I watched them, enchanted in the warm afternoon sun, as the talkative mothers took welcome dust baths in the dry soil. The young poults intermingled freely with other broods, yet at the slightest alien sound they would dart for the safety cover of their respective hens. How they recognised their mothers who all look the same is a mystery to me. Suddenly, the baby-alarm buzzed, the Pale Ale cask required changing and I reluctantly left my charges to the solitude of their own little world. I didn't realise that in the hedgerow opposite something else must have been studying the scene, for when I returned an hour or so later the sight filled me with a sickening revulsion. Sixteen Marans lay headless amidst the golden carpet of lifeless pheasant chicks; only a fox would commit such carnage as it played with its victims to the death. 'You bastard,' I screamed, shaking my fist at the hedges as my eyes began to mist. 'I hope the hounds tear you to pieces,' I muttered as I began to collect the carcasses. Then I realised that I was partly to blame for the massacre. 'Sump oil,' I murmured to myself. 'Engine sump oil.' Bob Styles and Uncle Ivor had always advised me to hang impregnated rags around the run. 'Fox can't stand the stuff,' they had both insisted. I'd used it the previous year just to stop them nagging me, but they were right, so right. What a cunning creature he was. I discovered his pawing marks where he had tried to burrow under the single sheets of corrugated iron surround, but they were buried a foot deep. I pictured his stealthy movement as he searched the wire perimeter for a hole, then he made one by clawing a rusted area and he was in. I sat on a tree stump utterly depressed, cupping my chin in my hands. I could forgive him for taking one to eat, but why this, I thought, this is nature gone mad. I couldn't sleep that night with the urge for revenge tearing at my soul. Just after one o'clock I loaded my shotgun. The late April night had a sharp bite of frost about it as I walked to the poultry sheds. I shone my torch along the perches, just a dozen Marans remained of the original thirty. No doubt that they would all go broody next year I thought, but I was completely dispirited. Just as well, was my false consolation, lot of hard work just for a crowd of toffs to pop off their shotguns. I laid a few of the headless Maran carcasses near the rusted hole of the wire netting, and sat down with my back against the henhouse and my knees to my chest. It was a half darkness from a starry moonless sky as my eyes remained fixed on the hole. Just his silhouette was all I desired, at thirty feet I would blast him to Hades.

Time seemed to stand still as I constantly checked my watch, and my cramped body grew stiffer and colder. Suddenly a faint outline filled the hole. The rapid increased speed of my heart vibrated throughout my body, and I wanted to stand to relieve the choking sensation within my dry throat. I quietly slipped the safety catch and raised the gun to my shoulder. As my open right eye scanned the length of the barrel and beyond I realised the shot would suffer the element of being wild. I prepared to pull both triggers on the moving creature as its eyes became more vivid. Suddenly its long thin tail went vertically erect as it created a mating cry. 'Blasted cat,' I murmured to myself while directing my torch-beam towards it. He was Ben, our large, over-sexed, old tomcat, out on the tiles for a futile mating expedition. 'That could have been your end, you randy old devil,' I said, as he rubbed affectionately against my trousers, oblivious to the fact that only the shape of his tail had saved his life.

As I lay in bed the following morning with a heart full of bitterness for the fox who failed to keep his rendezvous with death, the hunting horn echoed across the valley from Moulton. 'Get one,' I prayed. 'Get one and give him the same death as my Marans and pheasants.'

Only a week later poetic justice seemed to haunt me when Susan ran breathlessly into the kitchen as we prepared to sit down for tea. Her three friends eyed me eagerly from the doorway as she spoke. 'Dad, Dad, there's a baby fox up the middle lane, he's injured, can we get him and make him better and keep him as our pet.'

'Pet!' I exploded. 'Have you forgotten already about the Marans and pheasants. I'll be more willing to go up there and shoot it.' As her eyes began to fill, I realised I shouldn't have spoken that way, she was an innocent child free of the malice and hate that I carried; only too soon would she be an adult. 'Oh well,' I said after a minute of silence, 'dig up a cardboard box from somewhere and let's see what we can do.'

With my Morris Traveller full of village children who suddenly appeared as if by magic we arrived at the spot in the middle lane. She was still there, a pretty little vixen cub, panting with exhaustion and pain in the bed of ragwort near the hedgerow. She snapped feebly at my hand as I tried to lift her. You are being far too much of a martyr, I thought, as I made a second painful attempt to place her in the box. Turning the other cheek is a load of old nonsense continued my thinking as my sorely wounded hands placed the spiteful creature into the box.

'Let's go straight to the vet,' shouted Susan as I drove back to the Bells.

'Vet?' I blurted, fighting to suppress my outrage. 'I couldn't face the vet with that thing, he's a countryman, he knows of the killing they do, he'd think I'm bonkers.' A sea of dejected faces appeared in the driving mirror as a stony silence followed my outburst. 'We'll take her to the Barry Zoo,' I said, as their cold war tactics succeeded. 'They're used to handling sadistic savages like that,' and a row of broad smiles took over in the driving mirror. The twins Hughie and George – wonderful characters, who were showmen to perfection and eccentrics to the core – kept the private zoo. Hughie appeared at the small ticket office window with a large boa constrictor draped over his shoulders.

'He's not too well,' he said tapping its head with affection. 'He normally takes a whole chicken, then goes to sleep for a few days, but he's off both lately, must have something on his mind.' He ended with a laugh. 'What can I do for you?' He quickly diagnosed our patient as having two broken hind legs. 'Obviously struck by a car,' he said as he put the creature into splints. He commanded respect from all animals, and I was aware that the fox treated him far more tenderly than me.

The zoo was a poor profit-maker, and for many years the two men had tried unsuccessfully to obtain a financial grant from the local council to run the establishment. Their application was finally and irrevocably rejected when Hughie took a fine specimen of a Bengal tiger into the council chamber. 'To speed things up a bit,' he said later in court.

'What if we leave her here?' I said to Susan. 'Hughie will take good care of her.' A row of determined shaking heads was my absolute positive answer.

'Bring her back in a couple of weeks,' said Hughie as we made for the car. 'They should be mended by then.'

The potential little killer soon became quite a pet around the house, and I was thankful that Susan had sensibly christened her Red instead of the usual children's instinctive choice for such innocent names as Cuddles or Tinker. She took to following me around on my daily chores during closed hours, but I was most careful to keep her well away from the bar at open times, for my county customers would have considered a tame fox to be the ultimate insult, when they had to brand it as vermin to warrant the existence of the hunt in order to appease the growing numbers of saboteurs.

I suppose there is an occupational risk for any creature in being a pub pet and, with the exception of Ben the cat, who was a strict teetotaller, Red began to take her daily tipple along with Posy, our tailless ferret, and Lady, our sixteen-year-old Jack Russell bitch. Lady eventually went on to the ripe old age of twenty, possibly attributing her longevity to her daily noggin of Bells slops – in moderation – but Posy was a confirmed drunkard whom I discovered one day swimming happily in the bucket. Their antics in the bar after a session was hilarious, while Ben the cat looked on from his armchair near the fireplace in utter contempt, but I must confess that my wildest fantasy could never create a drunken cat.

The memory of the massacre, which would never be erased, was easing daily as my affection for the fox grew stronger. She followed me as I fed the stock, her eyes becoming as sharp as needle points at the sight of the Marans as she squatted low with a natural instinct to pounce. I habitually stared at the thick bramble beyond. Was her possible mate lurking in there? I experienced the feeling that a father has for his daughter on her first courtship. An attitude to protect her from the experience of growing up, yet I suffered a feeling of guilt and shame for the dead Marans and pheasant chicks. Suddenly came the impetuous maternal cry of my true offspring Susan. Like Toad of *The Wind in the Willows*, the world would have to stop for her latest desire.

'Dad, Dad,' she pleaded as she held a fluffy brown owlet to her chest. 'He's fallen from the church tower.' I suffered a repetition of the fox cub incident as her irresistible brown eyes and the trio of faces behind her forced me into submission.

'He doesn't appear to be injured,' I said after a quick examination, 'but how do we feed him?'

'Dead mice?' answered Susan with uncertainty. I made one of my pained expressions that usually had the effect of a few dozen words.

'I'm not going out on mouse-hunting expeditions. We'll have to create synthetic ones.' I remembered locating owls' perches in old buildings and barns by the little pellets of skin and bones of their victims that they regurgitated, and an idea entered my mind as I studied his pretty little face. 'The Marans to the rescue,' I said to the children. 'We'll chop up their moulting feathers with those little bags of chicken giblets from the birds we serve in the bar.'

With little concern for its unknown sex the children christened it Oswald and placed it on a perch near the eaves in a dark corner of the old stable. I fully expected the owl to reject our home-made feathered mice, but it gobbled them up eagerly, and began to grow quite strong. Within a few weeks Susan had introduced it to the other members of our hard-drinking menagerie, plus Ben the cat who still remained aloof in his sobriety.

Some weeks later a strange and sad incident took place as we all relaxed on the lawn during a warm Sunday afternoon. We looked forward to that day when the shorter drinking hours allowed us more time to ourselves. Sylvia was trying her hand at yoga and I was half asleep in a deck-chair watching through semi-closed eyes the children play with the pets. Stewart had discovered a length of four-inch-diameter plastic pipe with which he was training Posy to go down rabbit burrows. As he enticed her to follow a piece of simulated fur attached to a length of string, so did Lady try to follow her. She was a fearless little dog who suffered a serious lack of judgement, and we often had to dig her out from rabbit holes that were far too small for her. It was commonplace when out for a walk to hear her muffled bark coming from a narrow burrow where only her little stumpy tail could be seen wagging furiously about nine inches down. She managed to get most of her head into the pipe, watched in a very sober manner by Ben, when her barking awoke him, and Oswald who wouldn't venture from his new perch in the little dark out-building beyond the stable. Red studied the act from the shade of the lilac tree that was so heavy in bloom. She sat haunched with head low between her forelegs. Her tongue sagged from one side of her mouth, jerking slightly with her breathing, her eyes were glazed and sad. I put it down to the heat of the afternoon to which Lady seemed immune, as she reached from one end of the pipe to the other in competition to Posy.

Suddenly I became aware of the fox as she stalked in line with the hedges around the perimeter of the lawn and onto the car park. I could never really be at ease with her despite my affection. There were a dozen Marans free-ranging, and I could never trust her natural instinct to remain hidden and dormant under the guise of domesticity. Without disturbing the children, and Sylvia who had gone fast alseep in one of her postures, I followed her. Her movement was slow and indecisive as she walked along the hedgerow. She suddenly looked back to give me a feeling of guilty embarrassment of being caught out spying. She reached the henyard to look back once more as I felt Susan's hand in mine, her large brown eyes were shining with unbroken tears as she spoke.

'She's leaving us, Dad.' Such a simple phrase, but how it proved her positive acceptance of country life, when a town child would have demanded the animal to come back. Passing the Marans as if they were non-existent Red made for the bramble thicket with the slowest of movement, her ears erect, her neck outstretched and her tail straight. Something seemed to beckon her from within the thorns; we could sense her torn loyalty as she looked back to us for the last time with a pleading expression before entering a run in the bramble, as if to say 'please forgive me but I must leave you'. We turned to make slowly for the pub hand in hand. Our hearts were heavy with silent thought for the little fox cub of the middle lane. Many times after that when the hunt was in the area, I had a compulsion to stop and join their car followers who would be eagerly watching the chase from roadside hedgerows. Visions of my dead Marans would flash through my mind, and I wished the hunters luck and then I would see Red the vixen playing on the bar carpet with Posy and Lady, and my death-wish changed to a prayer of survival for the brave little creature who could induce such a frenzied cavalry charge of redcoats. But that was a country scene and, unlike the saboteurs, I felt that I had no democratic right to disrupt it however much I disliked it.

8 · Stewart's Special Brew

EACH TIME that I trimmed the hedgerow of the rear car park, I became more convinced that the Six Bells must have been completely self-sufficient at one period of its history. Wild hops grew in abundance around the perimeter to indicate that the area could well have been a hop field, while the various collection of out-buildings nearby provided evidence of a copper boiler and a fermenting vat. The situation could have been unique for we often searched the hedgerows of all the Vale pubs without finding a trace of the flower. Sylvia, with a gifted expertise in floral art, always displayed them in the bars along with sheaves of barley from the local farm, which could well have supplied the inn with its malt in centuries past. A map, drawn in 1622 by a cartographer with the most unusual name of Evans Mouse, shows little change in the village of the present day, and one can well picture the Customs officer dismounting at the Six Bells in that year to test the gravity of their home-brewed ale. Bartholomew Sykes had not then invented his hydrometer, and the only known method was for the officer or constable to pour a tankard of ale over a wooden seat and then sit on it; if the leather buttock patches of the officer's breeches stuck to the chair, then it was an honest brew.

The only building to suffer the ravages of time in the village was the Norman castle to the rear of the church, but I suspect that Cromwell had a lot to do with its decay. It did, however, conceal a modern-day treasure in the form of five hundred £1 notes in a wartime dried milk tin. They were discovered by a schoolboy archaeologist near a spot where I sat courting Sylvia on countless occasions. The origin of this treasure trove was pure conjecture on the part of the villagers, but they were unanimous in their belief that the treasure was the property of an old man who only left his cottage once a week to draw his old-age pension at the post office and then go on to the castle ruins.

The Bells' cellar was obviously the oldest part of the inn, only two steps below ground-level, with a grey flagstone floor constantly shining with dampness. The builder could never have envisaged that present-day beers are at their best in a temperature of 54°F, yet only in adverse weather conditions did it vary from that magic figure of perfection. During a heat-wave it would possibly rise to the middle sixties when the casks had to have a regular change of wet sacking overcoats. Arctic conditions were easier to combat by raising the temperature with an electric fire, but more costly. The higher the gravity of the ale the more fickle it became, and Hancock's Home Brew was a thoroughbred that demanded perfection in its keeping. If the conditions were not exactly right, it had a tendency to layer itself in the cask in cloudy and clear patches. As a barometer it was most effective in forecasting oppressive thundery conditions by turning cloudy, a habit not well received by the doubtful customer as he studied his murky pint. Contrary to popular belief, hops have no relationship to the gravity as alcohol is produced by the chemical action of yeast and sugar, but they do have the all-important function of preserving the ale and enhancing its flavour. The Worthington brewers at one time dispatched a small bag of hops with each cask of ale as an aid to its longevity in the cellar. It was the publican's task to administer these into the cask by removing the spile bung completely. The practice was only really necessary with slow-selling beers and most busy houses never bothered with the method, but we had one customer who could have warranted the function of dry hopping. He was our last remaining dark ale drinker in a growing era of light ale supremacy. No inducement or bar jibes would convert him from his lifelong choice of beer. 'Too much chemicals in that stuff,' he would reply to his critics. 'Sides that, it'll give you piles, 'ell of a lot of blokes whats gone over to that bitter tell me they got piles now, never saw 'em when they was drinking dark.' My problem was to keep his seemingly everlasting cask of dark ale in a drinkable condition. It was an easy beer to manage under normal stillage life of around four days, but even with the use of four and a half gallon firkins for his anti-pile serum, the livestock usually consumed a good remainder of each abandoned cask. I eventually persuaded him to drink the same brew supplied in quart bottles, to which he agreed under the protest, 'It's too gassy, could bring piles on with the strain.'

His fixation on the ailment was a standing joke and some time later that year when helping the farmer as a casual labourer he fell into the sheepdip trough while struggling to baptise a large reluctant ram. As he emerged through the white froth of the strong-smelling brown liquid someone shouted 'Bet that tastes better than the Bells' dark and it'll sort your piles out for you.' It is small wonder, however, that publicans must have immense shoulders to carry the insults directed at their beer. Some local landlords were past masters of the art of a witty retort when confronted with a complaint. One particularly renowned licensee of the area once replied to a non-regular who complained that the bitter was a bit thin: 'So would you be, mate, if you'd been dragged through forty feet of half-inch pipe.' To a customer who complained of cloudy beer, he held the pint to the light saying 'There's nothing wrong with that, just a dirty glass.' He remained undaunted when a high-ranking member of the brewery called in for a bar snack one day. Unaware of the man's identity he shouted through to his wife in the living quarters: 'Have you dusted the pasties and cheese rolls today, love?'

When keg beer began to replace cask-conditioned ale it made redundant the cellar and the skilled cellarman. The various systems of keg beer could be accommodated beneath the counter with absolutely no beer-keeping expertise required. The engine room of the pub became simply a stores. A far cry, thank heavens, from the days of lead pipe systems. It has been said that thousands of ancient Roman citizens died of lead poisoning because they made so much use of that metal in their water drinking systems. There can be little doubt that many of our pre-1950s beer drinkers died of the same cause for lead systems were the normal pipelines when beer engines were first introduced.

A popular story told during my licensed trade course related to the very conservative solicitor's clerk who was the first customer each evening at the pub near his office. For twenty years he drank just one pint of beer before leaving for home and lead poisoning was the cause of his death. It was a very hard system to clean and my father-in-law often repeated his experience when delivering beer to a large Cardiff hotel. A new stainless steel pipe system was being installed in the cellar, and as the fitters fractured the lead pipes a glutinous green snake-like jelly oozed out. The fitters quite nonchalantly informed him that all lead systems were the same inside. My father-in-law was more concerned by the fact that the hotel served the best flavoured pint of beer in Cardiff, which he enjoyed on many occasions. The stainless steel system reigned for many years, but when one considers the worst possible situation of beer being drawn from a cellar two floors below, through a hundred-foot length of twisting pipe and assisted by an electric pump, it is not real ale any longer, but similar to a central heating system. If we add to this dispensing method the infamous 'thrifty' valve on the beer engine it would represent beer serving at its very worst. The 'thrifty' valve, as its name implies, was a non-return pipe connecting the drip tray to the cylinder of the beer engine. Its function was to serve a certain amount of the slops into each fresh pint. It was an utterly filthy, unhygienic method in common use at one time in thousands of licensed houses throughout the country.

The decline in dark beer sales during that period was purely a consumer rebellion when they appeared to have spontaneously decided that all the slops and drainings could only successfully be filtered back into the dark ale cask, because of the colour. Every publican uses the filter, he has to when drawing off after pipe cleaning, or just prior to opening time when the systems should have been filled with water. My father-in-law, who visited many cellars in his day, was a strong advocate of not returning any dispensed beer to a cask, hence our fine band of alcoholic pigs. But, as Robert Burns noted, even the best laid schemes can fail, as when Stewart, my son, abandoned his babywalker and began to follow me into the cellar. On his chubby unsteady legs he watched my every move as I went about my cellar work. I was rewarded with a hearty handclapping applause each time I tapped a cask with the large wooden mallet and a brass tap, but when I vented a lively cask with the time-served engine valve to cause a spurt of beer as high as the ceiling, I would receive a dancing ovation.

The filter had an air of mystique about it that brought a serene expression to his normal happy features. I could well analyse his thoughts at the sight of the strange shining alu-

minium utensil with four legs and a long thin pipe that entered
the very bowels of the barrel like a scientific probe. It sat on top
of the cask like a thirsty creature from *The War of the Worlds*,
consuming beer by the bucketful, and giving out occasional
loud belly gurgles as the triple layers of paper filter allowed the
cleaned beer into the cask.

Stewart chose a Sunday for his experiment; he studied me
intently as I went through the daily brass-cleaning ritual of the
counter strip, the toilet pipes, the ornaments and finally the
front door handle. His interest intensified as I drew off the
water from the beer engines and pipes and then connected
them to the casks before pulling a bucket of beer from each for
the insatiable thirst of the filter. Suddenly the usual breathless
Susan ran into the bar, but with good reason. A wasp had
entered her mouth to sting her tongue as she ate an ice-lolly. It
was swelling at an alarming rate, and, with a real fear of her
choking, I dropped everything I was doing to rush her into
Barry accident hospital, some five miles away. I went straight
into an examination room without the formalities of booking
in, where a sympathetic doctor quickly gave her an injection to
ease the swelling.

Keeping a pub entails living by the clock, and while the
welfare of my daughter was obviously foremost in my mind, I
suffered a nagging fear that opening time was drawing peri-
lously close as I began the journey back to Penmark. Our
turnover would not allow an abundance of staff, and though
Sylvia had a full-time occupation with Stewart and her normal
household chores, the Saturday morning duty fell to me. Next
to Sunday it was the best morning of the week for trade, and as
I drove into the front car park ten minutes late to a sour-faced
reception of half a dozen potential customers, Sylvia in a
frustrated condition opened the front door.

'It must be the thirteenth,' she said forcing a smile at the
eager faces who brushed past her. 'I was just putting my face
right to come in the bar when Stewart, whom I'm loo training,
slipped backwards right into the damned thing. We'll have to

get him one of those little training seats, or we'll lose him altogether one of these days.' It managed to crack the frozen features of the irate customers, and the first pint received a smile fifteen minutes late. But time really is the nub of hotel management. People will accept poor punctuality in all its forms in reasonably good temper, but should their regular pub door open a minute late, they will throw up their hands in abject misery. Sylvia often told me the story of the Green Dragon Inn at Llancadle, a hamlet about two miles away. Her father received a phone call from the brewery telling him that the tenants of the inn had apparently walked out and left it like a *Marie Celeste* on land. His instructions were to break in on behalf of the brewery and begin serving until they could provide a relief landlord. Their main concern was not the obvious loss of trade at the small inn, but a fear that the mere handful of villagers who used it might collectively object to the licence renewal at the next Brewsters' Sessions. The true value of these inns to the brewery in those days was the capital asset of the property and not by the sale of their beers which was negligible in comparison to the equivalent-size town pub.

Every pub has its militant bar counter lawyer who is a self-styled expert in all facets of the trade from brewing to the law, and while he is quick to warn the licensee of his rights at the Brewsters' regarding the running of the pub, he is usually the worst offender in drinking up and leaving at closing time, which provokes the main threat of losing the licence in any case. True to Bob Styles' advice I stuck rigidly to the rules, for which I was very unpopular on that score, but I shall always remember the night when I felt like dancing along the counter singing 'I told you so'.

It was not long after the introduction of the ten-minute drinking-up rule. I called 'Last orders' at ten-twenty five, followed by 'Time' at ten-thirty and finally 'Your glasses please' at ten-forty. It was futile, I was utterly ignored, and with the nonchalant air of an actor I threw the glass cloth over and handpumps saying 'Thank you, ladies and gentlemen, I'm going to bed.' At that moment a police inspector, renowned for his over-zealous supervision of the licensing law, appeared in the doorway. The time was nearly ten-fifty. Most inspectors would simply have pointed at the clock; to him it was a cardinal sin. My dozen or so rebellious law-breakers sat stunned over their unfinished drinks like guilty schoolboys; I couldn't control the smug smile of satisfaction that came over my face. 'This is worth a fine,' I thought. 'They'll all go down with me in court. What an expensive, but sweet revenge.' The inspector gave me an impassive glare after looking at his watch and conferring with his sergeant as I tapped the counter with complete nervous abandon. The late drinkers remained speechless and frozen to their seats with silly little forced smiles on their faces. We were cornered like proverbial rats, all law-breakers, there was absolutely nothing we could do, the inspector held the cards. He walked over to the counter facing the miserable band of customers but addressing me.

'This will be recorded, Mr Brock, and I would advise you to be more vigilant of the licensing laws in future.' With that he left the premises to sit in the parked police car outside, obviously to await the rapid exodus of my little band of sheepish customers. My bar lawyer took command of the situation.

'Don't dare touch your drinks, and leave in the casual manner,' he said with an emotion that only the pigs appreciated as they consumed the abandoned drinks the following morning. In the immediate weeks after the inspector's visit the bar automatically emptied by ten-forty without any barracking on my part, but time soon erased the incident, and once more I was reduced to being the tyrannical bully of closing time.

I often discovered a profound wisdom in my father-in-law's reasoning of the utter impossibility of abiding by the law and remaining popular with the customers. At that period there still existed a number of centuries-old laws on the statute book, such as it being an offence to allow a customer to pay wages in a pub, or knowingly to serve a prostitute. I can well imagine the reply if I asked 'Excuse me, madam, but are you on the game?'

There can be little doubt that these laws were enforced for a sound reason in their day such as the payment of wages, when one can visualise a Dickensian scene of the drunkard recipient boozing away his family's sustenance money.

But under-age drinking has always been the licensee's nightmare where he is held responsible for assuming the age of the customers or bluntly asking them, and that can sometimes result in the most embarrassing situation, as in my case.

'A pint of Home Brew, please,' said the schoolboy character as he peered over the top of the bar one Saturday lunchtime. I took it as the ultimate insult to my authority.

'I'll give you pint,' I replied in temper. 'Where are your parents?'

'Over here waiting for my drink when you eventually serve him,' said the elderly man from the window seat. The little person at the counter with the rosy cheeks and wrinkle-free face smiled as he produced his birth certificate within a protective polythene folder. He was nearly thirty years of age. He accepted my apology in good faith, obviously being well versed in the predicament arising from his Peter Pan appearance.

A ludicrous situation arose one busy evening when a fifteen-year-old local girl was escorted into the bar by a chap of about twenty. Now the law states that a person over the age of fourteen is permitted into a licensed bar provided they are not served with drinks in excess of two degrees of proof, which is fairly weak, but as a futile form of exoneration and exercising my publican's prerogative of serving whom I please, I had a notice at the front door excluding persons under eighteen from the bars. In the eyes of the law I was still responsible for any under-age drinkers, but I felt that the notice may have been a deterrent to would-be offenders such as the village girl whom I immediately took to task.

'I'm only going to drink coke,' she replied with innocent youthful feminine charm. 'It's my birthday you see.'

During today's permissive climate, when I am informed that around fifty per cent of many pubs' customers are under-age drinkers, I would be ridiculed for taking the situation so seriously, but country inns were the essence of respectability in the 1960s. As the night became busier and the bar quite crowded, I lost sight of the girl who was holding court to three or four young men at a table near the window. True to her word she was drinking coke, but I was unaware that the double rums ordered within a round of drinks by her adoring beaux were also intended for her innocent coke. Suddenly, near to closing time, the usual busy conversation of the bar was stunned into silence when the girl broke into a hysterical fit as she fell from her seat to lie on the floor in a writhing convulsion. Immediately, I began to suffer stage whispers from some of my normally passive customers. 'Shouldn't have been allowed in in the first place, she's only a child' was the most popular type of verbal missile to reach my ears as I tried to help her to our living quarters. Her breath stank of rum while her glazed eyes and slurred speech indicated that she was nothing more than hopelessly drunk. I found it extremely difficult to control my feelings as I led her through the fickle-minded customers. When I refused to admit youngsters under eighteen I was nothing more than a miserable killjoy living in bygone Victorian days, yet when something like this occurred I was negligent. My opinion remains steadfast to this day. A publican is a very convenient whipping boy, caught between the law and his customers. He cannot serve both, therefore he cannot win the full respect of either. An innkeeper who consistently flouts the law will have a short career, yet one who abides strictly by it will enjoy a long but poor life behind his bar as in the case of Bob Styles. But they do have a shoulder to cry on in the form of the Licensed Victuallers Association, staunch and helpful allies. I personally requested their services on two occasions to receive prompt successful action which gave me a strong sense of security in an occupation where I was isolated from my fellow workers. Their daily newspaper, the *Morning Advertiser*, also keeps the publican in constant touch with the 'Trade', as it is known, and I found it to be a refreshing breath of enlightenment each morning in a strange little world of professional solitude.

However, I've sat on my bar stool for too long defending the poor licensee; let me return to Stewart and his experiment. The highly eventful Saturday morning came to a happy end with Susan's tongue returning to its normal size, and in good fettle to hound me. The customers began to drift away, but not before I received a highly honoured deputation from the bar lawyer and his committee. They were all suffering from slight over-indulgence, and I braced myself for some possible scathing home truths only to bask in egotistic pleasure when he spoke.

'You know, Derek,' he gently slurred as his index finger pointed in my direction, 'you know, I've been coming here before Bob Styles kept it, and that's going back a bit. Now, he had a good name for his beer, but this pint you're serving this morning, well,' he paused to lick the gummed line along his home-rolled cigarette, 'it's the finest pint I've ever had in my life. Don't you agree, boys?' he said, turning to his back-up team. The glowing praises flowed until my expanding head neared bursting point with the ultimate accolade: 'Nectar from the gods, man.' Trevor the Law then decided that the speech-making had made heavy demands on his throat, which only a pint of the magic elixir would soothe.

'Besides,' he said as the party returned fully recharged to their seats, 'a barrel of beer such as this one might never turn up again for a hundred years.' There was little doubt of their clever tactics to gain extra drinking time, and it reminded me of my father-in-law's tales of Bill Probert, the unofficial mayor and firewatcher of the village during the Second World War. He would tap on the door about midnight on numerous occasions, always with a sense of passionate urgency to his voice, and using ever-changing methods to exhort Bob Styles into parting with his precious supply of rationed drink. With the reputation of being the local sage, no one doubted his wisdom, least of all my father-in-law, who, he confessed, was the perfect model victim.

'I can see him now,' he would say, 'standing in the doorway, rattle in one hand, bell in the other. His firewatcher's helmet on the back of his head, all in readiness for the Penmark blitz. "We've had it, Bob," he'd say, "only a matter of time 'fore the invasion, I can imagine the jerry paratroopers now, dropping on to the back field before the week's out, the squareheaded sods. I s'pect they'll take this place over as a headquarters. They did in France in the last war, took all the pubs and cafés over, they did." He would edge his way into the building. "If you got a little drop of special tucked away, Bob, don't leave it for them buggers, 'cos they'll find it, an' have a good booze-up on your back, apart from that, they're nasty in drink, those Germans. You'd be doing the village a turn if you got rid of it before they came." ' The situation usually ended around four in the morning when the habitual all-clear siren moaned across the dawn countryside and two inebriated villagers went to bed happy in the fact that their supreme effort had deprived the enemy his victory drink for the invasion that never came. Bob admitted that he accepted the firewatcher's gloom lightheartedly and looked forward to the regular tipples as a form of anti-depressant, for the news was bad. 'But if the ruddy war had gone on much longer,' he said, 'I'd have been a raving alcoholic, for when things got better for us, he'd turn up to celebrate the victories as well.' Leaving my crowd of artful dodgers to finish their illegal drinks and crossing my fingers that the police would not decide to make a trip down the Vale, I returned to the cellar that I had so hastily vacated that morning. The filter on the Home Brew cask had all drained back, but what the devil was that horrible looking thing lying in the bottom? I picked it out gingerly, a large greyish-black rag smelling strongly of Brasso. 'Stewart,' I murmured to myself as I tried to recall the possible situation. 'He couldn't reach the filter so he must have placed the impregnated cloth into the bucket of beer that I had just drawn off to be filtered back.' I suppressed the desire to laugh aloud. 'They're as high as kites on the stuff and full of praise for it.' I could hear Trevor's well-worn and exaggerated gardening stories, but they were still good for a laugh.

'My father was the gardener,' he began to his appreciative audience. 'Grow anything he would. I remember when I was a kid up the Rhondda, before we moved down here, he used to walk away with the show prizes, carrots, they were his speciality. It shows the size of 'em when I tell you that the tops started to wilt in the garden one year. The old man thought it was leather jackets or wireworm eating 'em, but they were too far down for 'em,' his voice lowered to little more than a whisper before revealing the secret. 'And do you know what was getting at 'em down below boys? Pit ponies.' To a roar of laughter he continued with his anecdote. 'Had to use a cross-cut saw to fell the rhubarb, he did, and carry 'em home on his shoulder like a pit prop.' At that moment, as I returned to the bar, Stewart appeared in the doorway.

'Time, please,' he said shyly with his thumb in his mouth. His mother had obviously put him up to the ruse, but I wonder at that tender age if he realised the impact of his metal polish experiment.

9 · A Working Ferret

ONE OF THE ideal features of a good pub is a central bar serving several rooms. It offers immense savings in cost and labour. It is possible for just one person in the bar to serve all outlets when trade is slack during the early part of the evening, while the cellarman has only one serving area to stock up and service his draught beer dispensers. The Bells was most decidedly not this type of pub. It boasted two bars, but deviously separated by a flight of stairs to the bedrooms and a long passage from the front door. It was never intended to be more than a single public room hostelry, and the second bar was installed during my father-in-law's time. I well remember the dry Welsh Sunday that he chose to lay a beer pipeline from the cellar across the bar floor and hallway to the beer engine of the new bar. He would rarely use the services of the brewery maintenance department and thus avoid incurring the risk of having his rent increased by his old friend, the director. Unfortunately for me when I married Bob's daughter I also became part of the conspiracy, as his right-hand man in running repairs. The bar floor that I tried to cut through with hammer and chisel on that fateful Sabbath was definitely made from concrete not of this planet.

My finger knuckles bled profusely from wild shots of the hammer, and as the day wore on to its painful bloody conclusion, the swathe of bandage applied by Sylvia had worked loose so that my hands looked like those of a horror-film mummy. By teatime, we had excavated the trench and laid the four-inch-coil pipe in readiness to push through the plastic beer-pipe. After enjoying one of my mother-in-law's gigantic survival meals, we returned to the cellar, and began to feed the virgin beer artery on its vital underground journey to the lounge bar. With modest smiles of suppressed triumph we looked over our shoulders to the diminishing coil behind.

'Just like cleaning a blocked drain,' I said, but my words were premature. Our rhythmic movement jarred to a sudden stop as the stiff unpliant pipe encountered an obstruction.

'Bloody well guessed that would happen,' said Bob Styles. 'It's that bend turning from the bar to cross the passage, too severe.' We sat in deep thought for some minutes before I said something silly, purely to break the silence.

'Pity Lady wasn't a bit smaller, we could tie a length of string to her collar and send her through, then fasten that to a stout rope attached to the pipe.'

'Fred would go through there like a dose of salts,' said Bob. 'I'll go and get him.' He was referring to his large polecat ferret who did very little in the way of rabbit hunting, and obviously thinking the creature would eagerly wish to relive his youth with a trip along the outer beer-pipe. Not for the first time during my entry into his family I wished that Bob would accede to a rent increase and thereby place the onus of his numerous maintenance jobs in the hands of the brewery. I felt sure that he would enjoy the best of the bargain, but to him, the stubborn thirty-shilling rent had become an obsession of principle, and I continued to suffer in upholding it. He returned holding a tired-looking Fred in one hand and a ball of green silk fishing line in the other.

'Right then, Derek, you pull the pipe back out and I'll tie this to Fred's collar, used to be good in his day. I don't know what he's like now, mind you, getting old like the rest of us I s'pose.' He gave me the ferret. 'I'll go to the other end, and start sucking the back of my hand to make a rabbit squeal noise, then you shove him down the pipe, OK.'

The rabbit sound echoed surprisingly loud into the cellar, and I dispatched the eager wriggling ferret on his errand taking the fishing line at a good turn of speed. As Bob continued to suck his hand I estimated by the diminishing ball of string that Fred had reached his false quarry, but it was not to be.

'He's gone bloody shy,' shouted Bob from his kneeling position in the bar with no beer. 'I can just see his snout, the bugger's got wiser with age, he knows there's no rabbit at this end.' Fred's sharp pink nose suddenly appeared at my end of the pipe, and I hastily rewound the slack string. It is incredible how a ferret can make a complete about-turn in such a confined space, just as if his spine were made of rubber. He was obviously enjoying the game and raring to go after I gave him a good scratch beneath his throat. Once more the line paid out at a good speed as Bob sucked his hand, but Fred insisted on stopping just beyond his reach. I began to imagine the theory within his brain. 'There's something fishy here, it's not like the usual burrow, and the old man's acting the fool at the other end.'

One thing was certain, if the story had ever reached the brewery directors of a ferret installing a beer-pipe, Bob would never face them again. Fred began his eighth journey absolutely revelling in the frustration he was creating to the short-tempered humans at each end of the pipe.

'Got him,' bellowed Fred's master in glorious triumph. 'Now tie the line to that thin rope, make sure you do it well or we'll have to use Fred all over again, and the way he's acting we could be here till midnight.'

The blue nylon rope began to snake into the earth-pipe as I told Bob to haul on the fishing line, followed by the reluctant beer-pipe which again came to a sudden halt at precisely the same spot as before. Bob's richly descriptive vocabulary began to flow along the earth-pipe. The trouble was yet again the severe bend across the passage which the extremely rigid plastic refused to negotiate.

'Hot water,' said my exasperated father-in-law. 'If we shove the first couple of feet into a bucket of scalding water, that'll make it pliable enough to take the bend.'

In no time the defiant plastic capitulated into a soft malleable tube as the bubbling water forced it into submission. We both smiled with sadistic pleasure at the saddened spectacle of the once-proud pipe as we rushed to coax it around the infamous bend before it hardened. But it did, with a stronger resistance than ever. 'We'll pull the bugger through with my car,' said Bob with reckless abandon.

He was quite prone to such impulsive decisions with an average fifty per cent success rate and sometimes drastic results in the failures. The trouble was the restricted space in which the rather long old Rover had to do the job, her bonnet just six feet away from our neighbour's delicate old stone boundary wall. 'They reckon you can pull tractors out of ditches with this stuff,' he said of the blue nylon, as he fastened it to the rear of the car. 'Now give me a shout as soon as the beer-pipe appears, then I'll come back and we'll take another bite on him.'

Blue smoke belched from the Rover's exhaust as he took the strain in first gear and as the car came within a foot of the wall the reluctant pipe peeped shyly from its hole. As I waved my arms and shouted in triumph the blue nylon that pulls tractors

— but not stubborn beer-pipes — snapped, and the Rover shot forward to demolish Aubrey Bower's wall. He appeared in his usual, placid, unhurried manner, a complete rural contrast to his fellow urban type.

'I've been going to rebuild it for years,' he said with a broad smile. 'Now you've stopped me thinking and started me doing.'

Later that day in the company of Aubrey and Fred the ferret, we pulled through the first pint of Hancock's Home Brew in the new lounge bar. It had been a costly operation involving a demolished wall and a badly dented Rover, but Fred enjoyed a glorious day crowned by a saucer of beer that he lapped up with gusto.

Despite the innovation of an extra bar we had created more work and expense for the same amount of revenue. The pub rarely saw many customers until about eight o'clock, possibly less than half a dozen, but people just being people involved three using the bar, and three using the lounge or thereabouts. Before the new counter had been installed customers bought their drinks at the sole original bar and carried them to the lounge. So we had the option of employing an extra pair of hands throughout the evening or running endlessly back and forth between the bars. The obvious plan was to remove the staircase to another point and put a central bar in its place. The brewery, who now enjoyed a 'sensible' rent from me, shook their head at my proposal.

'The turnover of the Bells would never justify that type of expenditure,' said our supervisor. 'We've got really busy town houses begging for modernisation.' He began to mellow as I asked him to sample the qualities of his Company's products during one quiet afternoon at the Bells. 'Tell you what though,' he continued, 'these old inns are a bit of a liability to us. If you undertake to carry out all internal modernisation and maintenance over a period of twenty years we might issue a lease on a very low token rent.' I began to visualise the green of my father-in-law's envy when I told him.

'How much do I have to spend?' I asked.

He shrugged his shoulders and opened the palms of his hands upwards. 'About three thousand.'

I quickly compared it to the current price of an average semi-detached house. 'I'll have to talk it over with Sylvia,' I answered, 'but you can go ahead with all the preliminaries.'

He patted the side of my shoulder. 'Steady on, it's not so simple as that. It has to go before the Board. I'll ask the Company Secretary to put it forward, then we'll come back to you with their decision, but let me know your feelings before I do so.'

Sylvia showed a distinct lack of enthusiasm when we discussed the matter that evening. It was all too obvious that we had both been frogmarched into the pub in the first place, but while my affection for the inn had quietly matured, Sylvia still held deep-rooted memories of her lonely childhood there. I often sensed how she envied what she termed children from normal homes, how she spoke of the large Reagan family of Holly Cottage.

'Their parents had time for them. Mum and Dad did their best for me, but I was so lonely without brothers and sisters when they were in the bar.' Luckily our two children enjoyed each other's company but the bar also kept me from them in the evenings.

I won her rather weak consent to pursue the lease as we both felt we had burned our boats and to carry on with a successful exploitation of the inn was our only natural course. A customer and architect drew me a provisional set of plans for the brewery sanction and two months later I received a call from one of the directors. He produced a very lengthy and legal document with the typical fair-minded advice of his Company, saying that I should present a copy to my solicitor before making any decision. Then he stunned me with a verbal bombshell that immediately gave me a negative attitude of the whole affair.

'No doubt you've heard the proposed breathalyser law, Mr

Brock.' I had followed its progress in the *Morning Advertiser*, but I never realised its possible effect on a country publican. 'Only you can assess your proportion of car trade,' he continued, 'but I would say it's extremely high. We feel that country houses will suffer badly, while town pubs will increase their trade when drinkers are afraid to use their cars under the new law.' Once again I felt a strong sense of admiration and gratitude for his integrity. Hancock's confirmed my belief that they were a fine family company, considerate of the interests of their tenants. With the ominous yet unknown future effect of the breathalyser it would have been in their interest to hedge off a possible victim of the new law to me. The inn provided a reasonable living comparable to the national average wage-earner. There were numerous hidden benefits such as rent and rates paid for out of the business. Our food bill was absorbed within the wholesale account of the pub, while any possible expenditure for social purposes was virtually non-existent for we rarely left the premises, but when I divided the weekly earnings by the hours worked the answer was well below the national average.

These were my thoughts as I subconsciously browsed through the pages of the lease without absorbing any of its content. The whole purpose of the document had been my desire to create a considerable increase in the turnover of the inn, but the breathalyser posed the threat of diminishing it while leaving the responsibility of the premises in my hands for twenty years if I signed. The director appeared to have sensed my forebodings as we took our tea in the Bells' small living room.

'I suggest we shelve it, Mr Brock, until we have time to assess the full effect of Barbara Castle's law,' he said smiling. 'If when all the dust has settled, you feel that it would still be a viable proposition, then I shall only be too pleased to go ahead with the contract.'

In today's world of high-velocity business I doubt very much that his type still exist – more's the pity – for I harbour eternal respect for that man and his Company.

Monday 18 October 1967 was doomsday for country pubs when the breathalyser act became law. It would be sheer hypocrisy to condemn such a humanitarian method of suppressing senseless slaughter on our roads, yet publicans and drinkers alike cursed its introduction. I stoked the fires on that sharp autumn evening and awaited the outcome with considerable trepidation. Now Monday should have been my worst day for trade, but the historic date had not gone unnoticed by the villagers who arrived in force two hours early to witness the inn's downfall. Shirty was the first to arrive, fully equipped with a police protection plan, why I don't know, for he was a pedestrian, but all the villagers, I noticed, treated the affair with a holiday atmosphere within their mundane existence.

'If I keep posted in this window seat,' said Shirty, 'I'll be able to tell you when the balloon-blowers turn up to test us outside.' He was referring to the police, who were rumoured to be eagerly awaiting their field-day at every conceivable vantage point with their little blow-bags at the ready. This scare-mongering was completely unfounded with the exception of a few over-zealous officers who scrupulously used the equipment on every unlawful motoring query. Despite the healthy ring of my cash-till from the proceeds of the locals, there was a distinct absence of several car regulars, and those drivers who had decided to brave the law were definitely nervous in their drinking routine. Theories of various capacities per person were rampant around the bar with Shirty taking pride of place among the sages. He tapped the huge curved abdomen of a pork butcher from Cardiff.

'Now a frame like this could take three times as much booze as me and yet give the same reading,' he said to an audience eager for his humorous wisdom, but a motorist from Barry casually arrived to completely distract their attention when he produced a packet of continental breathalysers.

'Had these from a marine engineer friend of mine,' he said with a superior air as he placed them on the counter. 'Same warning levels as this country. The little tube of salts changes

'Well,' I answered, 'what do you suggest to make a few bob on?'

He tilted his tweed cap back with his thumb. 'There's nothing to beat a battery system for maximum results, but that involves a hell of a capital outlay to take away the cream.' He scanned the mixture of sheds. 'Knock all these into one and try a deep litter house, this place would take about five hundred birds.'

My enthusiasm increased. My conscience could tolerate a deep litter method where the hens, while confined to a building, roamed freely on a deep bed of wood shavings. With the use of controlled lighting and heat, the egg supply remained constant throughout the year, and the capital outlay in my case would be little more than the cost of the poultry.

'What birds would you recommend?' I said eagerly.

He was quick to reply with his favourite witticism. 'They're just like soap powders, these modern hybrids, everyone supposed to be better than the others, but they all lay an egg a day, so you pays your money and you takes your choice.' As if to confirm my earlier thoughts, he added, 'But go in for brown eggers, the public are fed up with white.'

I tried to inject some of my bubbling optimism into Sylvia when I persuaded her to work the morning bar session for me to which she agreed with a rather limp approval. Finance as usual was my stumbling block, but the cash surrender of a life insurance policy kindly provided the means to purchase five hundred point of lay pullets. With my usual and sometimes dangerous impetuosity the large shed was quickly made ready under the watchful eyes of the inquisitive Marans who were to have no part in the venture, remaining free-rangers and pheasant-rearers. The air was strong with the pleasant smell of mixed wood odours from the shavings as I viewed with pride the results of my labour. The food and water troughs were full, the new wire perches ready, and forty nest boxes of sweet meadow hay awaited their layers while the cosy virgin floor bed was ready for the constant scratching of a thousand feet.

I was rather disappointed when they arrived the following evening in a medium-sized van. My imagination had envisaged something on the scale of a furniture remover's vehicle.

'Best to have them this time of the day,' said the man from the hatchery, as he counted my precious £500. 'They'll go straight up on the perches, and think they've lived here all their lives in the morning.'

For a couple of hours after his departure I watched them emerge slowly and cautiously from the ten delivery crates. I tried to count them, but gave up in utter confusion to accept the man's assurance that they had been on the generous side with me.

That night I quickly sank into a deep contented sleep, confident that within a fortnight I would beat the breathalyser with my happy band of brown eggers. For a week I impatiently watched their combs grow into deeper shades of red as each day I searched the untouched nests for the first great egg, and then came two near disasters. The morning had a champagne freshness about it as only the country can, when I opened the front door to polish its brass fittings. From the valley between Penmark and Moulton came the excited shrill of the hunting horn and the hysterical baying of the hounds. Soon, as I put the final lustre to the shining door-latch, a metallic ring of horseshoes on tarmac began to invade the stark solitude of the village. I noted the serious faces of the riders as they trotted their sweat-sodden breathless mounts past the pub; they were intent on a kill. I thought of my dead Marans and I silently wished the hounds luck; then I pictured Red playing on the rug before the bar fire and I said a little prayer for her survival. By mid-morning, with my pub chores completed in sparkling readiness for the unrewarding first session of the day, I made for the henhouse to seek the elusive first egg.

Stewart ran on down the centre of the car park eager to be first in on the historic event, when a sudden bedlam took over to fill me with sickening fear that I have never erased from my mind, as a dozen or so mounted hunters emerged over the boundary hedge of the neighbouring farm. He screamed in confusion and terror as the hooves of the massive horses came within inches of crushing him into oblivion. I ran to his aid flailing everything with my empty egg buckets in complete futility and hurling useless abuse at the astonished hunters who were utterly bewildered to find themselves in a pub car-park. But a hunt will stop for no one when they are near to the kill and I had to rescue my son come what may. Pushing between the steaming milling horses I grasped his shaking little body and ran back towards the pub, where I thrust him into his mother's arms.

'I'll show them!' I said, shaking with rage, as I snatched my double-barrel twelve-bore from the gun rack. 'Who the hell do they think they are?'

Sylvia caught my wrist as I reached for the cartridge box. 'Now cool down, there's no need for those, just the sight of your gun will scare them off.' They were near the henhouse when I returned to hear my precious investment crowing in terror as the pack of hounds bayed at the bramble thicket nearby. I shouted at the whipper-in, 'I'll start shooting if you don't clear off at once.'

Luckily the situation resolved itself as the pack moved off to the cowslip field, leaving me to confront just three hunters. The man with the long whip gave me the impression that he wouldn't hesitate to use it on me, and I believe he would, but for the menacing barrel of my gun. They were guilty, there was little doubt about that, and they were eager to join the chase, but I demanded to be heard. 'You've trespassed, you narrowly missed injuring or killing my son and you've probably put five hundred pullets right off the lay. What are you going to do about it?'

Their patience was being strained to its limit. I was a mere distraction, a damn nuisance. They were rooted to the kill that was taking place not many yards away, where the exhausted fox had surrendered to the pack in a piercing death scream of agony, as the hounds tore at its body in victory. To deny them the spectacle after several gruelling hours of the chase was punishment in itself and they were deeply annoyed over my interference.

'Send your claim to the hunt,' said one of them as they spurred their horses away. To this day I abhor their arrogance. They sincerely believe they have a God-given right to pursue their quarry, wherever it may seek refuge, with little concern for the damage they leave behind them. But their hypocrisy is farcical to the point of lunacy when they claim that their prime purpose is fox control. Yet I well remember about that period a leader story in the local paper about a rather extrovert Vale of Glamorgan farmer. A photograph showed him standing proudly over a pile of dead foxes with a claim that he had shot a hundred in a month simply to settle the score for all the lambs he had lost. Some weeks later the same newspaper reported that his fox-hunting landlord had given him notice to quit! They would gain some measure of my respect in their defence of hunting if they admitted that their sadistic, destructive day out was purely for their enjoyment and not the eradication of the fox. Ironically, the eradication of the fox would put an end to their 'sport', but democracy is balanced on a knife-edge that the hunt-saboteurs must not be allowed to sway, for fanatics could champion various species right down to ants.

Most of my farmer friends said that claiming from the hunt was usually futile, so I suffered with clenched teeth the two-week delay the hunt had caused to my pullets, but Stewart did eventually find the first one and his success made his blue eyes sparkle as he held it to me. It was a pathetic little thing as all starter eggs are, no larger than a pheasant's, and soon I had buckets of them for sale at half the normal price. Within a few weeks they reached their full size, and we began to sell them over the bar only to discover a greater asset than their profit margin, when they increased the miserably reduced drink trade. As the news of our fresh brown eggs became established, so did a new clientele of townspeople emerge. They would call with their families and indulge in a few rounds of drinks before collecting their country produce. Their early evening contribution to the pub was a novelty but I soon realised that I was not catering for their children. They were bored and restless sitting in the cars. A 'Kiddibar' was the answer in the form of a large caravan which had been sited at the edge of the lawn for some years. I quickly converted the interior into a replica of the pub bar where I installed a very eager daughter and son as licensees to sell soft drinks and sweets. On the lawn I put swings, slides, see-saws and various small toys for the toddlers. It was a perfect site, safe from the road, where they enjoyed themselves in perfect harmony while their parents used the bar facilities safe in the knowledge of their children's welfare. But Susan's initial enthusiasm began to wane with the call of her childhood country life, and I could hardly blame her attachment to such rewarding interest.

'What if I take them on conducted walking tours while their parents are in the pub?' was her suggestion.

I shook my head laughing at her initiative. 'I can't see their parents agreeing to that,' I answered, 'and its turnover would never cover the wages of an adult, so the kids will just have it as a play area without the bar.'

But I was deeply concerned each time I made up the books for, contrary to the predictions of most people in the trade, the breathalyser continued to deter motorists from patronising country pubs.

10 · Mysterious Mushrooms

CHRISTMAS 1967 came as a pleasant relief from the trauma of the breathalyser, which had lost none of its initial impact. Car drivers were nervous – there was little doubt of that – as they watched anxiously the pedestrian villagers imbibe the spirit of Yuletide. For the first time in living memory the brewery allowed us the option of closing on Christmas night and, with a history of poor takings on that evening and two eager children to entertain, we closed our doors. There were warning rumbles from one or two stalwarts who claimed that they were not concerned over the loss of a drink, more so the infringement of their democratic freedom.

They obviously were little concerned for our welfare in taking one night off in a year, but Sylvia had decided to make the most of it, and it remains in my memory as the best Christmas ever.

The favourite upstairs room of her childhood, relieved of its dust, but still with its fusty smell, provided the perfect setting for our evening. The great log fire presented the warmth and illumination giving out that magic festive odour of roast chestnuts and burning yew wood. The children's faces beamed in the flickering light as we played our simple games, no electronic computerised marvels, just 'I Spy' and the like in an atmosphere unchanged for centuries. We even felt the presence of the celebrated Six Bells' ghost, and wished him well on such a glorious night when the village was as still as the churchyard beneath the sharp air frost of the clear starry sky; and the other inhabitants celebrated their rural Christmas in the same manner as ourselves. But problems never go away, despite the idyllic veneer of the previous evening, and Boxing Day saw their return even more intense when the seasonal followers of the hunt at Cowbridge Common were reduced in numbers.

My financial depression while working the bar that morning received an uplift when Shirty and Raymond arrived. They were deeply engrossed in the startling revelations of a Sunday newspaper regarding baldness and its dramatic cure with the use of chicken droppings.

'There's this bloke,' said Shirty to me as I pulled his pint, 'bald as a bat he was, and only a youngster like, and someone tells him to rub the droppings into his scalp.' I noticed Raymond, who painfully suffered a rapidly receding forehead, absorb this conversation intently. 'Within six months,' continued Shirty, after taking a liberal draught from his pint and sucking the fringe of white froth from his moustache, 'he had a full head of jet-black hair, and that's the truth if I was to be struck down now.'

'He'll take you at your ruddy word one of these days,' said Bert, the rosy-faced groom from the local stables, but the usual sarcastic reply did not come from Raymond, who remained deep in thought.

'Tell you what,' continued the undaunted Shirty, 'it grows mushrooms better than horse manure and they're strange things they are, full of cult and witchcraft like.'

'It could go wrong then, Shirty,' laughed another villager. 'End up with a fine head of mushrooms instead of hair.'

As the bar vibrated with raucous laughter, and Boxing Day took on its festive role, the seed of another enterprise was sown in my mind unwittingly by Shirty. Chicken droppings, I had tons of the stuff, not for hair restoring I hasten to add, but for mushroom growing – they would be a by-product of our egg supply.

As soon as the festive season was over, I headed full of enthusiasm for the public library at Barry where a gem of a book on fungi culture awaited me. The author had obviously devoted his life to the magic white buttons, and his book provided a detailed reference to every facet of this growth and, most important to me, the various composts in which they could be propagated. Contrary to popular belief that only horse manure would yield mushrooms, the author had successfully planted their spawn in every conceivable type of compost, including elephant droppings from a visiting circus to provide the best crop of his career. He went on to describe chicken droppings as a superb compost medium, subject only to the addition of urea, which it lacks. The essential ingredient had to be wheat straw and with three tons delivered along with an endless supply of humorous sarcasm from the local farmer, I set about the herculean task of producing my pyramid of compost. From the adjacent henyard the Marans looked on in awe as I constructed, in alternate layers of droppings and straw, my ever-increasing monolith of their colleagues' humble produce. As the height increased, my arms turned to lead and my stomach muscles ached with the constant pitching of the four-pronged dung fork. I took frequent opportunities, quite unnecessarily, to refer to the book that I fervently wished

I had never discovered in the first place. I was suddenly aware of an embarrassing intrusion as I mumbled to myself.

He was Raymond, who appeared sheepishly around the shed corner. 'Aye, Derek,' he said with his teeth firmly clenched to his pipe stem, 'd'you believe that rubbish of Shirty's, the chicken shit I mean?'

'Well, it was in the newspaper,' I replied, heartily pleased with the heaven-sent gift of a respite from the cursed monument of the foul-smelling stuff. 'But I suppose they'll print anything to sell the paper. Why, were you thinking of trying it?' I said tactlessly with my gaze fixed firmly on the shining half-moon of tight skin above his forehead.

'Well it's bloody worrying, eh?' he answered between a few sharp draws on the immovable pipe. 'I'm a fair bit off fifty, so I'll be as bald as a badger's arse time I reaches that age the way I'm going.' His vanity was a strong controlling feature of his character, and I was only too well aware of the nagging problem of his growing baldness. He removed his pipe for the first time after a few pensive movements. 'Oh hell,' he said with a forced smile, 'let's try a bag of it, I'll be the guinea-pig, and if it works we'll bottle the stuff under another name, make a fortune. You won't have to bother about the breathalyser then, just keep the place for the locals.'

As he walked confidently back along the car park with a soggy bag of droppings over his shoulder, I returned to my task with visions of a rosy future, where Raymond and myself were co-directors of a gigantic cosmetic organisation. Only one nagging doubt kept interrupting my optimistic train of thought as I continued to pile the potential hair restorer: what would we do about the smell? The heap had to be turned three times at ten-day intervals, during which it created enormous heat in a rapid decomposition, with my constant fear of it igniting by spontaneous combustion to completely destroy the fruits of my labour. But eventually it all turned into a sweet-smelling dark brown compost. 'Fit to eat' said the book and I laid the beds in a large disused shed between the pub and the lawn

'Then we came to the mushroom shed', continued Susan, 'and it's covered in little white pearls, honestly, Dad. Grampa had nothing to do with it this time,' she said with her stare fixed firmly on the old man who appeared stunned with her presentation of his poetic justice to a really innocent practical joke.

That time I walked to the shed as casually as my bursting excitement would permit, while the children danced along before me, and Grampa trailed eagerly in our rear. I suppose a veteran commercial grower accepts the sight as I saw it in a very mundane way, but to our four pairs of eyes it was sheer magic as the blanket of little white fluorescent peas seemed to grow by the minute in the semi-darkness of the old corrugated iron shed.

Customers rubbed their eyes in disbelief the following evening as I placed my home-grown mushroom sign beneath that of the fresh brown eggs.

'Wrong time of the year for those, surely?' was the stock phrase of most, who appeared quite ignorant of commercial mushroom production, believing they came only from the fields during the latter part of the year.

Like the eggs they brought trade, and for two months the rusted old shed provided a good crop every ten days, after which the bed was spent out and useful only as a garden compost, which I also sold quite fast to eager customers. But despite a constant demand, I found it most difficult to muster the energy for a second attempt and the venture faded away into a pleasing memory of a job well done.

However, I must mention the missing Posy. She was quite a small ferret, and tailless as her mother had chewed it away when she was very young. It was her minute size and natural sable colour that made her difficult to trace. Each night her meal of warm milk and bread was taken from her little kennel at the rear of the pub without a sign of the elusive creature. Her attitude was in strange contrast to her habit of following me around during my morning bar-cleaning and taproom work tobacco. 'My father told me about it, and I reckon it's done the trick. The old ram kicked and butted seven sorts out of him. Put him off sheep for the rest of his days I'll bet.' As he spoke Skip eyed him knowingly with a sort of sickly, grateful grin, and I could well imagine his thinking as 'Oh well, I'm battered and bruised beyond belief, but at least I'm alive.'

'Let's drink to that,' I said happily. 'And Skip can join Lady,' who was eagerly awaiting her morning tipple. Despite my No Dogs in the Bar notice, purely to keep their numbers at a sensible level, we did encourage the attendance of a few canine characters. There was Claude the poodle who took his nightly drink of beer from his personal ash tray and promptly went to sleep under the nearest chair, but as soon as 'Time' was called he wandered to the front door and howled until his owner left the premises. He was very much a licensee's friend and a stout upholder of the law. Then there was Bosun, a boxer, whose proud owner had trained him to howl at the counter for a pastie. This was all good pub entertainment during opening hours but the ever-hungry dog began calling at all hours to cry at the front door for an enforced free meal from me, which had a devastating effect on my pastie profits.

My various enterprising sidelines made a miserable contribution to the depleted revenue of the early breathalyser era, and in desperation after a visit to the accountant, I decided to look for a job, but first I had to request permission from the brewery to close on the weekday morning sessions. As usual they were most sympathetic to my case. The supervisor arrived unannounced on a Tuesday opening time to sit in the bar as an observer for the four-hour session, when my sole customers were Mrs Reagan for husband Danny's pint of draught and the local farmer who purchased his daily packet of small cigars. He suppressed a bored yawn as I closed the door at three-thirty.

'Well you won't make your fortune on those takings will you?'

'No, but it's been a pleasant change to have company,' I answered.

'I think you can begin to look for a job, Derek,' he said with a consoling shake of my hand. 'We'll turn a blind eye to you closing, but we can expect a few irate letters from people who might want to use the place once a year.'

And so I started out on my job-hunting marathon with a trail of negative results to indicate that something was dreadfully wrong. In most cases I was being rejected without an interview, which was a bit unexpected, and finally the truth was revealed by a very forthright sales manager who did see me in his London office.

'Your trouble is the address, old boy,' he commiserated from behind his large desk on which a portrait of his wife and children smiled sweetly. 'Wouldn't do for customers to know you kept a pub, bit unreliable I'd say, what?' I nodded my head in defeated agreement, knowing he was so right. The keeping of a country inn posed a fine status symbol, but only within the confines of the pub. Outside it carried a stigma if anything, eagerly referred to by such people as motor insurance brokers, who classed publicans along with actors for high risk assessment.

As the South Wales Pullman hurtled back to Cardiff I realised the futility of returning to a sales career while holding a pub licence. I felt the softness of my hands whilst the swaying waiter served the main course of superb Western Region grub. What a contrast, I thought, when your pick and shovel awaits you at Penmark.

Ray Vizard smiled along his firmly clenched pipe stem when I told him of my decision the following evening.

'Let's hope your future luck is a bit better than mine with the chicken droppings,' he droned. 'The old forehead have gained another half inch, and the missus don't want to know me since I started using it. I reckon that bloke in the paper must have had the stuff in his eyes to talk all that rubbish.'

Shirty was quick to correct him with his own brand of wisdom, which was completely ignored with an invitation to me for a game of table skittles.

Later that evening a local farmer and haulage contractor approached me at the bar. 'I hear you're going to close in the day,' he said. 'Fancy doing a driving turn for me now and again?' He was overheard by Raymond which caused me considerable embarrassment for I had arranged to start with him on the coming Monday.

'Give it a try, Derek,' he prompted in good humour. 'Bloody sight easier than the buildings, 'sides we want someone with the strength to serve a pint in the evenings.'

The farmer appeared to be a little too eager for my services. 'How about tomorrow then? Market day, that's when I need two pair of hands to drive the livestock truck as well.'

'Right,' I answered after receiving an approving wink from Raymond and a learned nod from Shirty. 'I'll be up the yard tomorrow morning.'

It required the services of our little-used alarm clock to rouse me at six the following morning, for the pub still demanded the same attention, and as I mopped the cellar in a martyred fashion I gained some solace to my persecution complex with wartime visions of Bob Styles. He had been excused from the forces by virtue of his being an innkeeper, but he had to take up work as a long-distance lorry driver under the Essential Works Order.

'Used to have this place all done by six in the morning,' he reminisced. 'Then take my old lorry with a full load to Manchester and back, to work here in the evening. I'd have been better off fighting, and away from the old woman for a bit.'

I arrived at the nearby Dermot Farm at eight-thirty where my lorry awaited me with what appeared to be a small load neatly sheeted with a tarpaulin.

'Just two drops, Derek,' said the smiling farmer as he approached me from the farmhouse still chewing the remainder of his breakfast. 'It's basic slag, ten ton of it, but don't worry – they'll unload it for you.'

At the first farm 'they' was a wizened little man with stooped shoulders well into his sixties at least, who instructed me where to carry five tons of the cursed fertiliser in tiny hundredweight bags. Building work can't be harder than this, I thought as I shouldered the last bag across the perfectly familiar farmyard and through the narrow doorway of the stone shed that waged a painful war on my bleeding knuckles. After a brief rest and clutching a shilling tip from the little old man, I made for my next call where 'they' was a middle-aged farmer suffering from angina and the after-effects of a recent hernia operation. I was convinced of his sadism as he supervised my carrying of the basic slag up a steep flight of stone granary steps for storage, and a seed of discontent began to nurture in my mind for my employer. But having gone so far I was determined to earn my full day's pay before telling him what to do with his job. His wife answered the phone in response to my call for further work.

'Pontypridd railway sidings, Mr Brock.' I thought she was highly formal to address her serf in such a manner. 'Go there for a full load of beet pulp,' she continued. 'Take it to Treforest Farm and that will be all for today, thank you.'

Once again there was no sign of the elusive 'they' at the sidings as I parked the lorry along the side of the closed railway van. Suddenly as I pushed the sliding door open an army of gorillas attacked me, for that is the only way I can describe a giant two-hundredweight hessian sack of beet pulp. I lay breathless as the avalanche of beasts pounded me to the lorry bed, and then, when the attack subsided, I began to off-load them. Once again it was like trying to dance with a gorilla as I embraced their massive girths in attempting to lift them. By this time my employer was the subject of a total hate campaign, and with darkness closing fast on the capital of the Rhondda, I roped down my towering load to confront the imaginary ogre of Treforest Farm. As I drove the truck in a wild temper at excessive speeds around savage hill curves, a picture of the beet pulp recipient was created in my mind. This member of 'they' would be an octogenarian in a wheelchair whose farm was inaccessible to my lorry by a quarter of a mile, while the store would be at the top of three very rickety flights of stairs. After risking the lorry springs along half a mile of cart track I suddenly found myself in the centre of a flagstone yard where the now familiar old man approached me with a tilley lamp.

'Here's your blasted beet pulp,' I snarled, 'Are there not *any* young farmers in this part of the world, or do they all run and hide when a good load arrives.'

I immediately prayed to withdraw my outburst as the bright lamp fully displayed him to me. He was a kindly old man nearing seventy, each of his old hard leather boots carried a criss-cross razor cut to ease his bunions, his baggy cord trousers were supported with a loose wide belt, and a set of button braces over his collarless Welsh flannel shirt. His lined face portrayed a long life of hard work.

'Only me an' the missus, I'm afraid,' was his answer. 'Used to have a boy we did, fine lad he was, but he died fore he was thirty with pneumonia like.'

I wanted only to vanish, but he took no offence at my terrible blunder.

'Let's have a cup of tea first, then we'll all pitch in, won't take long then like, will it, boyo.'

My volcanic temper soon subsided as I sat at the white, scrubbed table in the cosy atmosphere of their black-beamed kitchen, where framed embroidered psalms hung on each wall, and his wife fed me hot sweet tea and warm buttered Welsh cakes. Later, with my faith in human nature completely re-stored, I hurled the beet pulp gorillas into their store with renewed vigour, and bade farewell to these kind people.

But the venom for my short-term employer had returned as I reached the Bells after twelve hours of hard labour. My telephone tirade had little effect on him when I requested immediate payment on collection of his lorry.

'Haven't got the ready on me at the moment,' was his evasion, 'but I'll pop it over tomorrow.'

That weekend he mysteriously moved north to somewhere in Yorkshire, and I am still awaiting payment for the hardest day's work of my life, but an ill wind can sometimes blow good and I was destined to join Raymond's little band of workers in the most hilariously happy experience as a jobbing builder's labourer.

11 · The Jobbers

THE OLD disused chapel in the village centre was Raymond's stores and office where I reported for duty at seven-thirty on the following Monday. The Jobbers eyed me with a mixture of humorous suspicion, as we waited for the lorry and other workers from Rhoose. The fine old pitchpine rafters, that once echoed with the beautiful choral renditions of Welsh hymns, seemed to cringe in shame as the men freely used the descriptive power of their heavy language.

Soon we were on our way, some in the cab of the Commer, most of us to the rear under a canvas and wooden canopy hastily constructed by Spider the carpenter. We were the ultimate building machine, so I was assured by Shirty, as the ancient lorry bumped painfully along the unspoilt country lanes of the Vale.

'There's Lewis the mason and bricky,' he said pointing to the villager who kept clearing his constricted bronchial tubes with interspersed mumbling of 'Oh bloody hell, mun.' 'And he's Sid the plasterer,' he continued in a whisper. 'Don't wash much, but uses some cheap after-shave that he found somewhere.' The little man in the lounge suit speckled with pink plaster droplets gave me a wicked smile as he took a pinch of cheap menthol snuff from a battered tin.

'And he's Oliver, a good all-rounder, but a bit ruddy noisy,' he shouted above his high-pitched offering of the Twenty-third Psalm. 'Hellish religious he is, so watch your bloody language, he's as strong as a horse.' A very tall man who sat looking through his extremely long legs gave me a friendly smile.

'Jack's the name, used to be a bricky with the council, but I started here for a laugh.'

'You haven't told him your trade, Shirty,' said Bernard the driver from the open rear window of the cab. The truth emerged that he possessed no particular trade, but took a great pride in the unskilled occupation of laying drainpipes and digging cesspits, which is so much a vital service of country building work. His long-felt desire to wield the trowel as a professional bricklayer was never realised, for, in the words of Raymond, who allowed him many trials, it was generally agreed by all except Shirty that he and the tools did not mix.

Our first stop was at the site of a silage farm where Spider disembarked to make the roof trusses. At the next hamlet of Pancross, Lewis coughed and grunted his habitual 'bloody hell' as he prepared to repair a time-ravaged stone wall. Then on to the village of Llancarfan, set in a sheltered bowl of picturesque landscape. It was the era of the mass exodus to the country by townspeople who were obviously seeking a refuge from the hectic pace of urban life, when every building plot was eagerly taken and any old barn converted into a luxury home. Country jobbers, such as Raymond, with the expertise to carry out such work were at a premium, and his openly offensive remarks such as 'weird bloody townies' did little to deter them when in earshot.

We arrived at two very attractive Georgian-style houses which were nearing completion when he also appeared in his battered Ford pick-up. With his trilby cocked forward at a rakish angle and the immovable pipe clenched firmly between his teeth he presented the perfect picture of a gaffer.

'Aye,' he addressed us all, while looking up at the high chimney stack. 'You know what his lordship wants now? He wants a bloody concrete slab up there on top of the stack. Reckons it'll be traditional, stops the rooks nesting and draws the fire well he says. I told him it would cost another fifty quid, to try and put him off, and the silly bugger just says tut, tut. I tell you they're all bloody kinky are these townies.'

Jack, the tall bricklayer from the council, who I later learned was extremely awkward on his feet, stumbled towards him in a spreadeagle posture as he tripped over a brick. 'It's we're the ones who'll be kinky trying to get it up there, Raymond, especially with your type of scaffolding, a plank, two elastic bands and a safety pin, and that slab will weigh a few hundred-weight if it weighs a pound.'

Raymond's immediate answer was a prolonged smile before speaking. 'No matter what I provided, Jack, you'd ruddy well fall off it. Anyhow we got to do it somehow or other so Derek can make a start on it to break him in gently like, all right, Der? And watch you don't damage your pint-pulling hands.'

Nonchalance was a permanent feature of his character that belied his extremely thorough workmanship, yet all his employees were accepted as potential craftsmen until proved otherwise, as in my case, and I set about making the wooden mould for the controversial slab with eager enthusiasm. Later in the day, as I smoothed the creamy concrete to a fine finish, he reappeared on the site.

'That'll be the end of your artistic flair for the time being

Der, I got a little job for you up at Walterston, grab a pick and bar and a shovel and I'll show you where to start.'

As we d ɔve to the next hamlet he spoke of a farmer who was in his debt for roof repairs. 'I called there last night with Shirty,' he shouted above the rattle of the ancient Ford. 'And do you know what the sod did? "I got no money," he said, "you can take him." A bloody great boar, nasty-looking bloke he was. I was going to refuse when Shirty nudges me. "Go on, Ray," he says, "have him, I can handle 'em, and we'll make a mint in stud fees with him." Handle him be damned, when we got him to Penmark he went for Shirty and chased him all round the village, anyhow old Bill the piggery man had a look at him this morning, reckons he's so old, he's dried up and he'd be even too tough for sausage.'

We stopped at a traditional Welsh long house, dilapidated and ripe for the insatiable desires of the townies.

'Here we are then,' said Raymond. 'This is where you dig a little hole.' I followed him to an overgrown paddock some thirty yards from the building, where he paced out a ten-foot square placing a piece of broken twig at each corner.

'That's it then, Der,' he said brushing one hand against the other in preparation to load his pipe. 'Just dig away between the sticks.'

'How deep?' was my obvious question. He answered with his usual broad smile as he turned the ignition of the pick-up.

'Bit early to think about that yet, just keep going down, it's a cesspit.'

As the bark of his fractured exhaust pipe diminished into complete silence, I became aware of the tranquillity of the area, interrupted only by an occasional bird sound. I looked at the house while spitting on the palms of my soft hands for the marathon dig. Shirty had told me that spit was a lubrication to ease the friction of the shovel handle, but I suspect it's just a habit of labourers over the centuries. I completed the removal of the turf by mid afternoon to reveal a large square of fine brown loam. As I sat resting on the perimeter of the young pit my mind created a smiling face at each window of the stark empty house, and I began to feel demeaned with the realisation that the sole point of my labour was to provide a receptacle to accommodate their body waste. This feeling was to intensify throughout the making of that dreadful hole, and later that day, as I fought to remove the sticky, obstinate strata of bright yellow clay, the large watery blisters on my hands began to burst with their own painful method of shovel lubrication. 'So much for Shirty's theory' I thought while tying a handkerchief around my tortured palm, but soon the glorious sound of the Commer's horn relieved my depression, and as we headed for Penmark I believe I actually enjoyed the welcome sound of Oliver's Twenty-third Psalm.

That evening I was the subject of constant friendly ridicule as my bandaged hands served drinks and the general topic of conversation centred on fitness or – as in my case – the lack of it.

'They talk about the four-minute mile like it's a ruddy miracle,' said Shirty from his favourite prominent position of the bar's right angle bend, where he could be seen by his complete counter audience.

'Come off it, Shirt,' answered Raymond, as he aimed for the dartboard. 'Bet you couldn't do it in ten minutes.'

Shirty began to take on his nervous tremor as he took a generous draught of his pint before replying. He brushed the spilt beer from his suit lapels as he spoke. He had been thrown the gauntlet and he was playing for elusive time.

'How much?' he said as his right index finger cleaned the froth from his moustache.

'A quid,' answered Raymond after an endlessly long grin, followed by a rumble of surprise around the bar, for a pound would buy ten pints of best bitter at that time. There remained a stony silence with not even the thump of the darts or the clatter of the table skittles while Shirty looked into his half-empty pint as if it was a crystal ball to give him guidance. His outstretched arms reached the counter where his bony gnarled fingers strummed the brass edge nervously.

'Tell you what,' Shirty declared to no one in particular. 'I'l run from Tredogan Cross to the Bells in ten minutes and that's a good mile.'

The bar burst into a flurry of speculation, while Alf Young a Bells regular and professional turf accountant from Barry, seized the opportunity to open a book. The following morning as we set off once more from the old chapel for our daily labour Shirty appeared morose and immune to the constant baiting of his colleagues.

'Ought to be pacing us from behind, Shirty,' said Big Jack.

'Have to pack in the fags for a week,' leered Sid, while offering him his snuff tin.

Suddenly a cross-wind caught the canopy to take it on a maiden flight into a half-grown cornfield just as Oliver reached his top note with an ear-piercing pitch.

'Bloody well thought that would happen,' screamed Big Jack with his hands held tightly on his ears. 'You're not content with cracking wineglasses, you got to blast canopies off lorries.'

Spider the carpenter contributed his version of dry wit to the lively verbal foray as we carried the shelter back to the waiting lorry. 'I'll have to go back to the drawing board, boys,' he laughed, as we tried to walk carefully through rows of young wheat. 'I'll make it psalm-proof, Oliver, you're too powerful.'

That, then, was the light-hearted humour to prevail throughout the day where a few men worked together, but mine was a lonely task in that cursed cesspit where I had the macabre impression of digging a mass grave. The glutinous clay that stuck to my boots making them resemble the massive club feet of a Frankenstein monster, thankfully stopped about two feet below the surface in layers of limestone pinrock. My whole body vibrated as I attacked it with the long chisel bar, when it surrendered itself to me in countless strange shapes for the first time since its formation millions of years before. My painful bleeding hands took a welcome relief from the shovel shaft as I threw the freed rocks to the square perimeter, and but for that sole discomfort my body began to tingle with the exuberance of a long-lost fitness. At one o'clock my cheese sandwiches and bottle of cold tea appeased a ravening hunger like food for a king as I sat near my hole and listened to the sounds of the country from rubbing grasshoppers' legs to the raucous crows tending their young in the sparse-leaved elms above me. It was all so very much alive in the growth season of spring, but death stalked where predator took predator and man chased the preying fox with the shameless tone of his hunting horn as I listened with the serenity of a man with a full stomach. I became aware of a heavy panting breath to my rear, and in broad daylight I felt afraid as I turned my head slowly to confront a large liver and white hound. His long frothy tongue lolled to one side in rhythmic jerks with his breathing as he approached me cautiously. What is he like with humans, I thought, this pack creature who knows little affection from man and tears a fox to pieces with all the savagery of a lion? His straight tail began to wag slightly as I held toward him, resignedly, my remaining piece of afternoon cake which he swallowed without so much as a taste, but it sealed our friendship and he squatted near me in deep affection as I patted him.

Soon his graceful strong head nestled between his fore paws in deep sleep and I returned to the pit, trying to fathom the mystery of his appearance, as I tackled yet another layer of the neat virgin limestone. The still air was disturbed with the thump of horse hooves and a feminine voice as I looked up to an attractive young huntress, immaculate in her black habit astride a chestnut hunter.

'Nero, you sleepy old rascal,' she spoke in her expensive, clipped accent. 'So this is where you have been all day, is it?'

The hound licked his jowls and rolled his eyes upwards in a guilty acknowledgement of his disobedience. It was the first time I had encountered the female of the hunting species, and I must admit I found the combined odour of horse sweat, saddle leather and her own perfume disturbingly sensual and provocative.

'We missed him quite early in the day,' she continued as she dismounted. 'Would you be a good fellow and find something to tie him with? Hay cord will be fine if it's available.'

All my prejudice melted away rapidly as I jumped from the pit to go to the stable at the side of the house, where I had seen some bales of hay. She walked at my side in easy conversation, utterly feminine and charming. What Jekylls and Hydes make up these hunting people, I thought. Just like the lovable docile hound who trailed behind us, she would enjoy the horrible gory death scene of a hunted fox. No doubt she had been initiated at the pagan blooding ceremony of her first kill, where the severed tail of the unfortunate beast had been soaked in its own warm blood and brushed across her pretty mouth. She viewed the interior of the building as she tried the door.

'On second thought this will do fine, there'll be no need to tie him. I'm sure the owners won't object to my locking him in here until our kennel man calls for him.' She tried the rusty bolt to reassure herself. 'Yes, this will be fine, many thanks for your help.'

As she rode away leaving me numb with her beauty, that vivacious yet ruthless killer, my mind became more rational as I compared her with the vixen who killed my hens; perhaps in her world she was just as perfect as the woman who smiled back and waved to me as she left the paddock. 'It's all a vicious circle' I consoled myself as I returned to the pit. From her earliest years she had been bred to accept fox hunting as normal as breathing, while I found it alien to my nature because I had not received the same upbringing, so once again I confronted my mental brick wall on the subject, and the answer is just as obscure to this day.

The news of Shirty's race had spread well around the Vale, and the Bells became quite busy with punters and inquisitive onlookers of the challenger, for at forty-five and being a smoker and drinker of considerable volume he could hardly be classed as the all-round athlete. He possessed a dogged will that would see him along the undulating mile and a quarter from Tredogan Cross to the pub. In truth, very few villagers ever considered the road to be any form of an obstacle, for it was a fact of their daily life to walk it morning and night before the use of the car, but the feat lay in Shirty's ability to complete the course in the critical ten minutes.

As Alf Young lengthened the odds for a victory to the runner a date was fixed for 6 p.m. on the coming Saturday, and I made the immediate decision to phone the brewery for an increase in my beer order to cover the event. The following day saw the arrival of the new owners of Walterston House as I peered over the edge of my hole, which was then a very proud five feet deep.

'I hope they realise this bloody thing isn't completed yet,' said Raymond during his mid-morning visit. 'They're not s'posed to be in for another fortnight, typical townies, all hustle and bustle like there ain't no tomorrow.' He tapped his pipe on the heel of his boot before a refill. 'Come to think of it I haven't started on all the other jobs she wants done.' He squatted low from the wind to light up the fresh tobacco. 'You haven't done bad, Der, but we'll have to have a couple more hands in there, and the house. S'pose we better have the whole gang over here to make a start this afternoon.'

As I sat on the edge of the pit at lunchtime Raymond's client approached me with a large steaming mug. She was a pleasant woman, not then in her forties.

'Would you like some of my kidney soup?' she said, offering me the cup. Now I have discovered that people generally either take offal with relish or reject it completely, and I am one of the latter, but her well-meaning invitation was extremely difficult to refuse, and I forced myself to swallow in her presence what was to me a most objectionable liquid. My problem persisted when she assumed that I enjoyed the beastly drink and I suffered a regular dosage of it for many weeks to follow, as well as the constant remark from Raymond that she was building me up for something.

But she also became a keen student of Shirty whose strange form of wisdom she found irresistible. As the cesspit neared completion with the brickwork of Big Jack in readiness for the building inspector, I was transferred to the task of demolishing an old stone annexe of the main building, where she approached me as I attacked the putty line bonding of the walls with a long chisel bar. Her eyes followed Shirty who was filling the concrete mixer nearby. She kept her voice low as she handed me a pearl necklace.

'They're just a cheap imitation string, drop them between the stonework and shout for me when you pretend to find them. I'm dying to see Shirty's reaction.'

I allowed a few minutes to lapse before going into the act.

'Mrs Manning,' I called urgently, 'come and see this.' Shirty was at the scene before her to study the semi-concealed pearls with an extremely learned expression to his face before scratching away the surrounding particles of stone and mortar with his nicotine-stained index finger, that ended in a permanently split nail. He pursed his lips to suck the air through his teeth pensively as he slowly withdrew the necklace with all the careful skill of an eminent archaeologist.

'You know what these are?' he said with a questioning tone, while holding the string in his two cupped hands for our perusal.

'Bloody pearls,' answered Raymond. 'Any silly sod can see that – sorry about the language, Mrs Manning, I'm always putting my bloody foot in it.'

Shirty gave him a lowering glare in continuance of their strained relationship of the pending race. 'How they come to be here I mean,' he replied with a superior air. 'All the eighteenth-century masons wore them, must have dropped off this old boy, when he was building this very wall, I can even see where the clasp broke.' There followed a dumbfounded silence from the circled audience, not for the revelation, but in Shirty's audacity to create such an obvious tall story which was quickly

exploited by Raymond.

'What yer saying is that all the masons of that time were bloody queers, a load of old bullshit I reckon – sorry about the language again, Mrs Manning.' But she had already left for the house aching with suppressed laughter and quite unable to reveal the true story to Shirty who, as usual, had convinced himself of yet another of his ill-conceived theories.

The building inspector called that afternoon to inspect the new drains and cesspit, as Shirty stood by nervously drawing on his cigarette and Raymond covered his movements from a concealed position in the stable.

'Can't stand that bastard,' he repeated constantly. 'Bloody trouble-maker, that's all he is, waste of bloody public money. I bet they haven't got them in Russia.' Despite being the ultimate conservative he habitually referred to that country as a Utopia.

As the Inspector's assistant pumped bright yellow smoke into the neat line of glazed clay pipes, so did the great man study each joint for the sign of a leak. Finally, he looked into the cement-rendered cesspit before signing his approval and drove away without having spoken throughout the exercise.

'Is he gone?' asked Raymond from the stable doorway. 'Ignorant sod, could have said goodbye.'

Shirty was quick to seize his opportunity. 'How could he say goodbye to someone who was hiding from him?'

But Raymond had the last say. 'I only keep away from him for his own safety. I'd hit him otherwise, the bloody Hitler that he is.' He spun around suddenly as he walked toward his pick-up. 'Better put that blasted slab on the stack at Llancar-fan, can't ask 'em for a dram till we've done that. Lewis and Derek better come down there with me now and we'll have a go at it.' The unexpected news brought on a coughing attack to Lewis but with the aid of a few 'bloody hells' we soon arrived at the scene of the dreaded chimney ascent.

'Good job we left the scaffolding up,' said Raymond, shielding his eyes against the late afternoon sun as he looked up. 'Just rig up the pulley and rope, and we'll hoist the bugger up.'

'Not a hope in hell,' said Lewis with a cough as I began to climb the ladder with the rope tackle over my shoulder. Soon I had the pulley fastened to the highest steel tube and allowed the rope to snake down to the men below who tied it to the much-vilified slab of concrete.

'Now half a little minute,' said Raymond with his favourite phrase. 'Let's have a little think on it. Lewis, you get half-way up the scaffolding to pull it in for a rest, 'cause we're not going to do it in one, that's for sure, and Der you come down and pull on the rope with me.' Lewis coughed and swore his way past me as I descended and soon we were ready for the hoist. 'Right,' said Raymond with the traditional spit on his hands, and seemingly naked without his pipe. 'Up she goes.' With the creaking rope searing into our hands and our heels dug in like a tug-o'-war team, the stubborn slab slowly ascended skyward and its first stop near Lewes. 'Pull him in, Lewis,' gasped

Raymond. 'Pull him in for Christ sake, or down he'll come again.' There followed the welcome slackness of the rope as the violently swearing Lewis completed his task, and we sat on the grass to compose ourselves for the final lap of the operation. 'I better take a bite round my waist now, like an anchor man,' said Raymond, 'this last bit is going to be a bugger. Right, Der, take the strain, and you ease the slab gently over the side, Lewis.' There was a sudden whistling sound like a descending bomb followed by an excited cry as Raymond was snatched from the ground, and the slab landed near his vacant space with a heavy thump. When I looked up he was suspended by the waist like a limp rag doll dangling in a slow-spinning circle. I found it impossible to contain my outburst of laughter but he hung there completely unperturbed until he faced Lewis, who was nervously clearing his throat with an obvious expression of guilt. 'I said ease the thing gently over the side, Lewis, not drop it like a bloody ship's anchor. Now go down and give Derek a hand to lower me a bit quieter than the slab if you please.'

His first duty was to his pipe as he reached terra firma, but as he assessed the drama in silence, while I dried my eyes, and Lewis continued to cough and swear, he decided to abandon that particular project.

'We'll get Spider to knock up a bit of shuttering and make it up there,' was his verdict through a cloud of smoke as he lit his precious pipe. 'I don't fancy going through that bloody flying lark again, on the other hand we could call Shirty in to work out a theory.'

The man in question, however, was conspicuous by his absence at the Saturday morning session of the Bells the next day.

'Where do you reckon he's got to then?' said Raymond as the wall clock struck two. 'He must be taking it serious to miss out today and not even having a bet on the horses by the look of it either.'

'The man's going to be a jibber, that's for sure,' said Bert from the stables. 'He's gone into hiding, we won't see him here anymore. He'll use the Green Dragon at Llancadle from now on. Won't be able to face us, he won't.'

But he was wrong when I heard a knock on the rear door at five-thirty that afternoon to reveal Shirty. He was dressed in his usual well-worn suit, complete with collar and tie and in no possible manner could he be compared with a runner except for his footwear. On his left foot he wore a black plimsoll, while his right side looked quite ridiculous in an over-sized once-white, tennis shoe. He drew long and hard on his cigarette in reaction to my surprise at his appearance.

'Used to have a pair of each round the house at one time, but the bloody dog must have had 'em.' He turned his head both ways to assure himself that no intrusion was imminent. 'Tell you why I called, I don't s'pose you could sell me a drop of whisky to relax me like, no good having a pint, I'd be stopping all the time.'

He followed me into the bar where I gave him a double malt on the house, a good investment for his crowd-drawing return in my favour. As his gnarled hand showing the scars of countless injuries held the glass with a tremor to his mouth, I became even more aware of his remarkable character. He was a Walter Mitty person whose fertile imagination just led him from one embarrassing situation to another. I believe his tremor was purely the outward symptom of his self-inflicted stress, but behind all his bravado was a heart as soft as putty, and I can never recall a word against him. At ten to six his volunteer chauffeur arrived in our fast-filling car park to drive him to the starting point. With glistening eyes and a steady hand he swallowed his second double with an acid wince and a low wind noise before going outside to tumultuous applause by well-wishers. The bar quickly filled five minutes before the legal time and the healthy ring of the till was music to my ears after the long, arid period of the breathalyser. A cavalcade of vehicles trailed Shirty from Tredogan Cross while those that overtook him gave me a report on his progress to the great interest of Raymond, who leaned on the counter near the window forcibly trying to completely ignore the episode as if it were non-existent, but his eyes betrayed him with their constant fixation on the wall clock.

Susan suddenly squeaked to a halt on her cycle shouting excitedly into the bar from the front door. 'He's just passing the farm everybody, and he's looking awful and sweaty.' Her words were drowned in the sound of clapping hands and verbal encouragement as Shirty rounded the corner looking even worse than Susan's description.

'Twelve minutes,' said John Henderson, the official time-keeper, as his car followed close behind. It was some time before the runner was able to speak as his chest rose and fell like a blacksmith's bellows, but he did manage to consume a full pint of bitter between the heavy breathing. For one glorious evening the Bells returned to a pre-breathalyser atmosphere and a wonderful spirit of goodwill existed when it was generally agreed that no honour had been lost by Shirty, who finally retired to a corner seat with enough drinks to his credit behind the bar for many days to follow. The frigid relationship with Raymond also melted back to an argumentative norm but only for a limited period when, yet again, Shirty followed the compelling instinct of his imaginative mind.

He tapped the pub side window the following morning as I began to clean the bar. 'Do you fancy a Sunday turn?' he said at the door. 'Time and a half, it's worth a few quid, 'sides that I got no one to drive the lorry for me.'

I had a mammoth backlog of work to clear in the pub and the smallholding, but I felt honour bound to help him. 'It's only over at Dermot,' he said with a broad smile in realisation that he had won me over. 'That new set of drains is blocked already, and there's a few other odd jobs that will take up the rest of the day.' Within five minutes the old Commer was dropping down through the steep road of the woods to Cuckoo Mill, over the Weycock river bridge and up the narrow hill to Dermot Farm. In a state of neglect for many years, it had recently been purchased by a local farmer who required only its land. Consequently, after a complete renovation by Raymond he had let it to a young business couple. One of its new features, like so many of the Vale properties at that time, was the provision of a cesspit which had barely been christened by virtue of the blockage to Shirty's new line of drainpipes.

As I unloaded the lorry of our various equipment I watched him feed the cane drain-clearing rods into the inspection chamber near the house.

'Still blocked,' he shouted over to me as the last section of rod was inserted. 'I'll go down to the pit to see if they've come through.' I watched him lift the iron manhole cover then lie on the concrete top to look inside. Suddenly there was a loud gurgle as the trapped sewage at the house end of the system was released, and Shirty's head was quickly withdrawn from the cesspit.

'Bloody women,' he spluttered, wiping his face on the arm of his coat. 'No drain can take them things.'

I exhausted myself with uncontrollable laughter at the sight of the whole incident, and on reflection I realise that I have never enjoyed such mirth as my time with Raymond and Shirty. The money was poor, the work was extremely hard, but, my goodness, they were stress-free halcyon days. He decided to take breakfast after spreading his sodden jacket to dry on the pit top.

'That's your job, Der,' he said through a mouthful of bread and cheese, with the green end of a spring onion protruding like a cigarette. 'That row of concrete posts, we got to put a wall there instead, so you gotta dig 'em out an' put a cement footing in their place. I'll see you later,' he continued, walking toward the house. 'I got a bit of craft work to do up here.'

He returned at lunchtime to continue with the same menu as his breakfast, followed by a cigarette. 'You're going great guns, Der,' he said through a swallowed spasm of wind as he replaced the cork into his half-bottle of cold tea. 'I got a slow old job up at the house or I'd be down to give you a hand.'

The following day while taking our lunch break at Walterston House we were paid a visit by Raymond who was hellbent on making a spectacle of his cousin.

'Aye, Shirty,' he called from a distance, ensuring that we would all be witnesses to the ridicule. 'You better not go near Dermot anymore.'

'What d'you mean, Raymond?' he asked with a guilty expression.

'You know what I mean, Shirt,' came the reply. 'The dry wall that was in front of the farmhouse, they thought the bloody world of it until you goes an' tries to point it, an' makes a hell of a mess of it.' Raymond's leer was transformed into an acid smile as Shirty squirmed and he continued with his verbal onslaught, which prompted me to eye Shirty with certain misgivings. 'I didn't say nothing about touching that wall. I said call for Derek and between you dig out the old posts and lay a footing for Lewis to build a stone wall. Evan the farmer is very annoyed, I can tell you, reckons he's going to take a bit off our bill for buggering his wall up he says. It's a hell of a good feature ruined.'

Shirty was utterly stunned, it was the only time that I could ever record him being speechless, as Raymond continued to flail him with a final death-blow to his already wounded pride. 'You better go over there, Lewis, and try an' tidy it all up, and for God's sake, Shirt, stick to what you're best at, cesspits and drains.'

He was morose for the remainder of that day, and how we missed the forthright revelations of his strange fantasies, and the more unusual episodes of his past life. But it all returned the following morning when Melvin the apprentice discovered an adder as he removed a long-standing pile of bricks. Shirty was quickly on the scene in response to his cry.

'Nothing in them things,' he said as the boy warily tried to move it along with a stick. 'India's the place for snakes,' he continued as he picked it up with a superior flourish, only to dispose of it quickly as its head surged up towards his hand.

'Now, if that was a cobra we'd all be in bloody trouble.' All work at Walterston came to a halt with the hint of a strange story of the east as his audience composed themselves in eager anticipation. 'In the RAF I was at a fighter station near Bangalore,' he began with a serene expression of satisfaction. 'Now the toilets we had out there were chemical, like they have in the caravans nowadays. About six of them, there were, in a row of little huts. Anyhow I was on my own one morning, enjoying a good one, when the bloody great cobra rears up in front of me with a head like a frying pan. The cheeky bugger had come under the six-inch door gap.' The countless wrinkles of his weather-worn face took on their smiling feature as his mind searched the past for fact or fiction. 'It's just as well I was on the bog with him staring at me all ready to strike. "Shirty," I said to myself, "one move and you've had it, 'cause he'll go for your throat faster than your missus goes for your pay packet on a Thursday night." ' He waited for the responsive laughter to subside before continuing. 'The trouble was my fag end. It was burning my fingers something chronic, so with my eyes fixed on his I lowered my hand slowly between my legs. I can tell you there was beads of sweat on my forehead as big as raindrops as we stared at each other. Then I drops it into the pan. Well, I don't remember much more except a feeling of going up through the roof in a sheet of flame, cobra an' all like.' We were dumbfounded in waiting to hear the conclusion of the mystery, but we had to wait until he had rolled his cigarette, and as he licked the gummed edge of paper the sage went on. 'I came to in the sick-quarters where I was treated for burns and shock, but that was better than being done in by that flat-headed sod.' He lit up the crude cigarette. 'And do you know what caused it? The ruddy bog wallah who couldn't read English had poured petrol down the pan instead of chemical, but it saved my life, and that's the truth if I was to be struck down now.'

12 · Rising Damp

IT IS DIFFICULT to select a favourite season if you are a
country dweller, each has its own distinctive attractions.
But, as far as a country innkeeper is concerned, summer has
the edge over the others for it brings a notable increase in the
pleasant ring of the cash register thanks to the family trade.

The breathalyser posed little threat to those parents who
spent generously on soft drinks and snacks for their children as
they enjoyed a modest glass or two of beer. My job with
Raymond thankfully arrested our financial decline, but there
were times through utter fatigue that I sadly considered giving
him notice out of physical necessity.

'There's no need to kill yourself,' was his reply when I broached the subject, but the building industry, like farming, waits for no man and I struggled through the month of August 1967 in perpetual exhaustion. Several arrangements were made in my favour for an easier life at the Bells, and one such move was my posting to a job just two doors away, where we were carrying out extensive renovations. Rising damp was one of its acute problems, a malady completely alien to Raymond.

'I don't know why these townies is so fussy about a bit of damp,' was his sermon one day when the new owner instructed him to eradicate it. 'All ruddy cottages got it, that's the novelty of living in the country,' he continued with a strong hint of sarcasm. 'You're bound to have it without a damp course. When I was a nipper you could tell the season by the way the wallpaper stuck to the wall or not through damp. Still, I'd better ring around to see if some smart aleck can cure it.'

Two days later there arrived a smooth-talking consultant in response to Raymond's inquiry. Like a myna bird he repeated word for word his apparent newly acquired sales jargon as he assessed the gravity of the problem. Raymond trailed him with a cynical expression reserved for all salesmen, as he made entries within a very impressive folder. He began to condition his client for the pending verbal estimate as he prodded the wet plaster with a small instrument.

'Pretty bad, Mr Vizard, it's reached the height of at least four feet, but we can bring it down to ground-level and contain it within six months.'

'How much?' requested Raymond through a puff of smoke along his pipe stem. The question was quickly evaded.

'What we'll do is this, Mr Vizard.'

'How much?' persisted Raymond. 'I don't give a damn what you do as long as it's cured, but how much for Christ sake?'

The young man's features took on a pink flush.

'Well it's not a cheap system, Mr Vizard. The installation is highly technical and the sophisticated equipment is very expensive, but as you would be the first in the area our charge would be four hundred and eighty inclusive.'

The blood drained from Raymond's face. 'Bloody hell, it's not so far back when you could buy a cottage for that money, but the bloke wants it done, so that's that.'

The salesman quickly produced a contract for his signature as he offered him a black plastic pen with his company motif on the barrel. His hands were raised in a display of generous refusal as Raymond returned it.

'With the compliments of the company, sir. We'll make a start tomorrow, good day.'

Raymond gave me a weak smile as his car pulled away.

'Hope it works, hell of a lot of money if it don't. Mind you, no wonder they can give pens away.'

Sylvia appeared in the doorway holding Stewart's hand. 'I'm off on the egg round now and I've left a salad in the fridge for our lunch, and for heaven's sake make sure you lock up when you leave.' Her side glance caught Raymond holding his hands to his ears. 'You don't know him as I do, Ray, he trusts the world.'

A rumble from my stomach prompted a check on my watch, and I made for the Bells as she left accompanied by Raymond's humorous condemnation of the fair sex.

As I began to appease my ever-present builder's appetite I heard a car arrive at the front of the pub. Despite the legality of our morning closure I suffered a pang of remorse that we should be shut and I listened in nervous silence as they tried the door in utter disbelief that a country inn should be closed. I consoled myself, as I heard the two car doors slam in obvious temper, that I had probably lost the profit of two half-pints in addition to my own enforced drink, purely on medicinal grounds as an anti-boredom serum. There is nothing more depressing to a publican than a bar with just two customers who isolate him completely from their conversation. With nowhere to escape, he repeats work that has already been done, while humming or whistling a silly self-composed tune to avoid the stern glares of the whispering couple, who class him as a nosy intruder to their conversation.

Two other inns had joined me in morning closure – the Mason's Arms at Llanbethery and the Green Dragon of Llancadle – but the brewery were satisfied in the representation of their products at the Three Horseshoes of Moulton and the Fox and Hounds of Llancarfan and this was pointed out in reply to the few letters of protest received by them.

Mrs Reagan changed her venue to the back door for Danny's precious pint, which he enjoyed to the very end of his life, and as no other villagers required our services during the week there was little inconvenience inflicted on the local community by us.

The following morning saw the arrival of the damp-treatment technician from Cardiff. At least that had been his profession for three weeks prior to a varied career including a slaughter-house assistant and encyclopedia salesman, he told us, as he spoke with muffled tones through his dust mask during intervals of drilling one-inch holes into the stone wall near the floor.

'That's the secret of the system there in that box,' he said through a cough, 'even I don't know what's in it.' We peered through the swirling dust of his labours to a black steel container about a foot square. 'It's all to do with the capillary action,' he continued. 'When I've drilled these holes, I thread a copper wire through them and back to the box.' He noticed Raymond's puzzled expression. 'Capillary action is just a posh way of saying rising damp, mate. Anyway, that box or whatever's inside it stops the capillary action and the damp stops rising. Got it?' We nodded our approval above the deafening rattle of his masonry drill and adjourned to more peaceful areas of work, when Sylvia appeared once more to say there was a pie in the oven for my lunch.

'And don't forget to lock up,' was her parting instruction, as another load of eggs departed for Barry with Stewart waving from the rear window of the little estate car.

Later, as I sampled her excellent cooking with gusto, I was

aware of the rapid staccato chattering of magpies. I adore the antics of these fascinating birds, and I rushed outside to the source of the commotion where a beautiful large ash tree grew like a sentinel over the rear of the Bells. Two magpies were hopping excitedly from bough to bough, completely unperturbed by my appearance, but on closer inspection, I noticed between the foliage that Ben the cat was the object of their attention. As he held on precariously to a bough far too slender for his weight, they wheeled and cried trying to force him to the end with the intention of making him fall off. Eventually their strategy was successful as he dropped in perfect cat fashion to the branch beneath him amid a chorus of an even louder victory chatter by the magpies. But they definitely resented Ben in their tree and the act was repeated four times until he steadfastly reached the final bough before the ground. As he looked behind with true Dunkirk grit, he made the decision to evacuate with a successful and traditional four-feet landing. I thought that would have been the end of the encounter but with a few friendly brushes against my legs he scaled the ash once more to confront the playful birds who welcomed him with a renewed outburst of chatter. His newly discovered game of death-defying acrobatics lasted until the autumn when both parties objected to playing in a bare tree for some reason.

When we left the Bells about fifteen years ago, Sylvia brought with her one of its tiny self-germinated offspring to plant in the garden of our new home. This summer it is a fine graceful tree, some twenty feet tall, but only a few days ago as I was writing these very pages, I heard the familiar chatter of two excited magpies. Looking through the window, I saw our third-generation Ben, a tabby cat, in exactly the same situation as his predecessor being forcibly ejected by the feathered tenants of that ash tree.

Looking at my watch, I realised that time had also flown at the rear of the Bells, and I raced up to the cottage about twenty minutes late where the cement mixer patiently awaited my attention. It was extremely difficult, however, to absorb Shirty's theory that mixers emanated from the days of the pyramids' construction, but only Raymond ever had the audacity to challenge his pronouncement, while others accepted it light-heartedly.

As I switched off our machine the light summer air carried the melodious tone of a male voice choir from the direction of the Bells. Someone enjoying records or the radio in their garden, I thought, but who? The couple next door were out all day and beyond the pub lived Aubrey Bowen, a definite non-musical type. I was drawn to seek out the mystery as I walked down through the village as far as the Bells, where a large coach was parked. From the half-open door of the inn came a fine choral rendition of the beautiful Welsh tune, 'Myfanwy'. My mind rushed back to Sylvia's constant reminder about locking up, and I hadn't done so, but how could I blame Ben and the magpies for my negligence? The driver smiled tiredly as I woke him from his catnap while walking past.

'You'll have a job getting served in there, they're a thirsty lot.' The combined sensation of annoyance, panic and humour took control of me as I dared to visualise who might be serving them.

'Been here long?' I stammered.

'No, about five minutes at the most,' he answered. 'They're a rugby club on a day trip to Barry Island, but this is as far as we've got – they can't pass a pub.'

I rushed up the stairs to pull a sweater over my cement-splattered shirt before entering the deafening atmosphere of a crowded bar. It would be utterly futile to try to tell a rugby club from the Rhondda that we were closed during the day – their minds would never comprehend such a fantasy – but who wants to be closed to such trade, I thought, as I confronted them at the bar.

'Sorry about this,' I gasped through heavy breathing, 'I've been doing a bit of cementing round the back. Don't usually see many in the day.'

'That's all right boyo,' said their spokesman. 'First things first, we were all bursting, so we haven't lost no drinking time, have we boys?'

A chorus of agreement answered him as a little man returned from the toilet carrying a black bowler hat crammed with various money, and a passage was quickly cleared for his approach to the bar. 'Thirty-two pints of bitter if you please, landlord, and a glass of lemonade for our driver, poor fellow.'

As I pulled on the pump with my cement-grimed hands I thought of the mixer: I hadn't washed it out, a cardinal crime in the building industry. And Shirty, Big Jack and Curly, had they missed me? Or was I so insignificant? The situation was so unreal, it had all the ingredients of a theatre farce, yet it was so very factual. I was working myself to the point of physical and mental exhaustion just to subsidise an old inn that had never really made a profit. No one could live more frugally than my in-laws – they were the essence of thrift – but they had retired to a rented cottage with very little capital.

As I served the second round of thirty-two pints and a lemonade for the driver and the woodworms sought refuge from the high-decibel rating of 'Bread of Heaven', Shirty, Curly and Big Jack appeared in the doorway.

'Three on the book, Der,' shouted Shirty. 'That damp bloke is choking us all up there.'

It was four in the afternoon and two hundred pints later when I managed to lock the door behind the thoroughly inebriated bus party, not to mention the six lemonades of the bored bus driver. As I rushed across the car park after ensuring the door was well and truly locked, Sylvia drove in. I quickly fabricated my lie, for I could never admit my negligence following all her warnings.

'I opened up for a coach party, well worth it too, must have got through two kils nearly.' Her first priority was to clean up the bar for the evening, as I returned to the scene of my first labour.

The damp-course technician had retired early from his drilling and I capitulated to my nagging desire to open his mysterious black box. Shirty immediately joined me in the drama as we set about the lid with a star screwdriver.

'There'll be one of those new computer things inside, you mark my word,' he said confidently. 'Amazing things they are, just like a human brain, but a thousand times better. Trouble is, that it might get out of hand and take us over, that's the danger.' He moved away from the box as I started on the final screw. 'Watch yourself, Der, could be full of radioactive cells, or something queer like tha. . .' His authoritative conversation came to an abrupt halt as we stared at the contents in complete disbelief. 'It's, it's a bloody battery charger, that's all it is,' spluttered Shirty. 'You can buy them for less than three quid. Well I'm blowed, they've taken Raymond for a ride, have that lot.'

He was the first to break the news to his cousin in the bar that evening.

'Well that's one for the book, eh?' replied Raymond. 'By the time they drill the holes and wire it up to that thing I don't s'ppose the whole job would come to no more than fifty quid at the outside, the robbing sods must have seen me coming all right.'

The consultant arrived at the cottage the following day as we took our lunch break. Raymond greeted him with a difficult, forced smile as his eyes remained focused on the all-important document case under his arm.

'Sorry for the dust and incovenience, gentlemen,' he said waving his trilby hat to clear the density of pollution before him. 'Just two more holes to drill, then we'll complete the wiring. Should be finished by tonight.'

But Raymond was not his usual self, remaining silent and extremely observant of the consultant's every move, when suddenly he made a very contorted wink in my direction. 'Fancy a little drink then, Mr Er . . . ? I'm sure Der will open up for us, won't you, Der?' I nodded my approval, while trying to guess his motive. 'You can leave your stuff just there, Mr Er . . . Shirty will keep an eye on it won't you, Shirt?'

There is a strange illegal sensation about serving in a closed pub during permitted hours; perhaps it is the fear of being discovered by a genuine customer who is astounded to find the place closed, but the consultant was most certainly bewildered over the whole affair when a builder's labourer drops his tools to open a pub, then ushers his two customers to an unseen corner, where, with a keen observation of the window, he deviously serves their drinks. I had the distinct impression of his thinking that we had broken into the place, for he was most uncomfortable and eventually very pleased to return to the cottage, where Shirty met us with a wide smile on his seasoned face.

'Your bloke's finished the job and gone,' he said to the consultant. 'He said it's all wired up and working.'

'Ah good,' replied the damp expert opening his briefcase. 'Now if you will be so good as to give me a cheque for the full amount, Mr Vizard, in return for your copy of the contract and twenty-year guarantee, the transaction will be complete.' His face grew into deepening shades of red as he searched for the document, watched by Raymond and Shirty with the silliest of expressions. 'Well that's most strange,' he said with a sigh of defeat. 'I could have sworn I put your documents in my bag this morning, but don't worry, I'm sure they're safe and sound back at the office, and I'll call with them tomorrow.'

The two conspirators broke into laughter as his car pulled away. 'I'll set you up for a bender tonight, Shirt, but what did you do with the contract?'

Shirty made his customary clicking sound with his pursed lips. 'Where else, Raymond, but the cesspit.'

The consultant called the following morning with a new contract but Raymond refused to sign.

'I've changed my mind mate,' he began to the worried man. 'It's a lot of money just to keep a bit of damp down, I think you'd better tell your bloke to come an' dismantle it.'

The consultant's unruffled charm was quickly transformed into a fiery temper as he stormed towards the tell-tale black box to sever the wires with a furious snatch. 'I'll just take this, Mr Vizard, you can have the rest with our bloody compliments. There's more in this than meets the eye. Contracts don't just vanish from my case.'

Raymond watched his car wheels spin with excessive acceleration as he tore from the site, before shouting up the staircase to the carpenter, 'Aye, Spider, there's a car battery charger in my van, knock up a little box for it. Do a good job on it, and make sure no nosy buggers can pry inside it, like.'

A few days later the new owner of the property called with his wife to view our progress. He was a townie according to Raymond, who branded every male wearing a collar and tie with that tag, but his wife was very attractive, which caused him to moderate his language and sound his aitches in the wrong places.

'I must say you've done a wonderful job, Mr Vizard. Hasn't he, darling?' said the man as he paused in his inspection near the impressive little box of Spider's creation. 'And this is the magic box you were telling me about, is it?'

'Aye,' replied Raymond to his wife. 'That's supposed to do the trick for your damp, mind you it's a waiting game, you won't really know the effect of it for a year or so, but here's the guarantee should it fail.'

'You took a gamble giving him that, Raymond,' said Shirty, as the couple left.

'I don't think so, Shirt,' said Raymond as he placed an advance payment cheque between the sweatband of his trilby. 'By the time he finds out if it works or not that ruddy firm will be out of business. They can't last long, a gang of cowboys like them.'

And how right he proved to be when those so-called specialists of damp and woodworm eradication just vanished into oblivion within twelve months, leaving him five hundred pounds richer. Shirty made an everlasting issue of the incident by saying whenever they had one of their frequent differences 'I put you where you are today, Raymond, by nicking that contract,' and Raymond would reply with his cynical laugh 'Well you had nothing when you first came from Llantwit Major to Penmark'. The argument invariably took place in the bar where Shirty would earn roars of laughter with his well-worn answer: 'Aye, an' look what I've worked my way up to now, a bloody bike.'

I realised as the various local inhabitants portrayed their characters that the breathalyser had put the clock back thirty or forty years when the sole purpose of the Bells was to serve the villagers. As autumn began to shade the village into its colourful rustic hue I was also aware that the law had been in force for a whole year, and it wasn't, as my father-in-law said, 'a nine-day wonder'. The weekly account book carried the same depressing message with monotonous regularity to inform me that our takings had remained at a fifty per cent decline since the introduction of the Act.

'This is absolutely ridiculous,' I said to Sylvia, as I closed the account book with a bad-tempered thump one Sunday afternoon. 'We're just slogging ourselves into early graves for less income than the average labourer.' I was on my soapbox and felt the need to impress my wife, who was always reluctant to change no matter what cross we bore. 'We're not giving our best to the kids,' I continued as I spread my hands to display the cluttered table. 'Just look at this lot. There goes our Sunday afternoon when we could all be enjoying a good walk in the woods like normal humans.' As I collected the books and various paperwork I recalled the words of a Cardiff publican some years previously when I called on him in my capacity as a cider salesman.

'My father-in-law keeps the Six Bells in the Vale of Glamorgan,' I said with pride and a tinge of snobbery as we stood at the end of a very busy bar, where the staff weaved between each other and the till bell rang its monetary tone non-stop. He turned around to face his customers with arms folded as he answered me.

'Aye, they're like snow, are those places, all right on Christmas cards, but no good in reality. Just look at this lot, they're the salt of the earth, nothing fancy, and half of 'em have seen inside prison, but they spend as long as the pub's open, and they give me a ruddy good living.'

'We're just part of a Christmas card,' I appealed to Sylvia, 'log fires, shining brass and copper, but no one spending anything, it's no good, we've got to admit defeat and get out.' She nodded her head in a weak gesture of approval, but it gave me the credibility to look for a reliable job which was the first step of our exit from the Bells. Once more the stigma of my address scared off prospective employers and our existence continued to be subsidised by the revenue of the egg round and my earnings as a builder's labourer.

I sometimes felt during the lighter moments of my jobbing that life could be idyllic in that vein if only we had somewhere to live, but the Bells was like a tied cottage, only willing to house us as long as we worked for its owners.

The rapid decline at that time of real ale, as it is now known, gave promise of an easier life with the simple management of keg beer, but until the time of its complete demise the same loving care and attention had to continue. It's ironic that the beer-drinking public caused the death of the ale that they now so much crave. Pubs proudly display large invitations to try their real ales, when just a decade ago they wooed the drinkers with a publicity drive on their keg beers, but the consumer calls the tune and cask-conditioned ale received their thumbs-down in favour of keg beers.

The Bells remained a conventional beer house because of my lethargic attitude. Time and again I had tried the various money-making options open to me to make good the losses inflicted by the breathalyser until my patience was exhausted. I was not alone in my plight. Several neighbouring inns changed hands regularly, but there was always a constant queue of applicants on the brewery waiting list who thought they could make a better show of it than the current licensee. They usually succeeded for the first few weeks when customers would forsake the bars of their locals to study the newcomers, but once their curiosity had been satisfied they rarely returned. The mildest vibrations of my discontent sometimes uttered in the bar were enough to provoke a flood of applications to the brewery from opportunists who craved my 'lucrative' roof. Some didn't trouble to conceal their aspirations and openly discussed at the counter plans for the improvement of the business. Others would remain silent throughout the evening in a deep study of our every move and totally unaware that we knew of their intentions. But customers in general are like a bag of dolly mixtures with their varied personalities and attitudes to pub life. Some regard their local with the same patriotic fervour as a football fan, ever loyal but quick to criticise any considered weakness of its administration, from the stocking of a new line or a slight change in decor. We once lost the custom of a very good regular couple from Barry. For many years their thrice-weekly visit had continued in perfect amity with never a complaint. We were obviously concerned over the loss of their trade, but also mystified as to the reason until a 'floater' called.

This is a person who appears regularly at several pubs with precise timing. He is an eager news-bearer, usually bad news to the recipient. Ours was no exception. His smug smile forewarned us. 'Saw Jack and Edna over the Dragon tonight, seen a lot of 'em elsewhere come to that.' He knew the reason for their defection, and I was dying for him to continue as I virtually rubbed a hole in the counter before him in anticipation. I served four rounds before he revealed the cause of offence. 'It was that new fag machine of yours that did it,' he blurted out eventually, as I hovered near him once more. 'Didn't like it right from the start, he told me, then he lost a half-crown in it and that cooked him altogether like.'

I was stunned to realise that he would forsake his local of many years over a cigarette machine, as I glanced into the hall where the chromium monster stood. In my current financial depression it was an absolute necessity, for cigarettes showed a miserable profit margin in return for an outlay sometimes larger than the drinks bill, but they were a customer service and when the vending machine operator proposed to relieve me of the costly responsibility I hastily approved. I should have viewed my profits on an average basis but my impartiality was often thrown to the wind with high esteem for the more lucrative wine and spirit drinkers. Soft drinks came surprisingly high in the range of profit-makers, followed by bottled beers, and finally, despite their constant demand for loving care and attention, draught ales. Contrary to their popular image I discovered that darts players contributed the least profit while placing the most demands on the pub's facilities. Their slowly consumed beers remained flat and lifeless as they played on with relentless enthusiasm. Their loud applause of a winning shot sometimes caused more studious drinkers to cringe with held ears, and the amount of room they absorbed finally turned their meagre profit into a loss. With these facts in mind, and dreading the possible outcome, I removed the dartboard and replaced the throwing area with three tables and twelve chairs. It was an immediate success and obvious proof that extra drinking space was the only real answer to the breathalyser, for the simple reason that I needed more customers now that individual consumption was limited.

My elation was short-lived when a devoted darts player from Barry arrived. He was a nice enough person, despite his profit-value to me of around two shillings a week. I felt decidedly uncomfortable as he methodically prepared his darts with cool precision and an expression of serene pleasure on his face for the impending game, oblivious of the pristine circle of wallpaper at his rear where his beloved dartboard once proudly hung. Ever a creature of habit he sampled his pint with a small sip and turned slowly around to face the high altar of his pastime. He swirled back quickly to face me with an ashen face, his hands grasping the brass edge of the counter to steady himself, his normal passive eyes straining wide in utter disbelief. The words failed to form in his restricted larynx and I

began to fear his next action.

'Whe. . ., where's it gone then?' he said with the limp smile of a practical joke victim.

'Sorry, Fred,' I answered as I forced a nonchalant wipe of the counter. 'A matter of survival I'm afraid, I needed the drinking space, darts take up a lot of room you know.' The explanation fell on deaf ears, for I've long discovered that non-business types will accept no excuse in the name of profit; to them it is a dirty word to be treated with scorn, and just like the farmer who constantly swims in a slurry pit of debt, the publican is dismissed with the ever-popular phrase 'You never see a poor one do you?' I wonder how far you go to impress the public. My father-in-law always said 'Never have a decent car, or they'll swear you're making a fortune out of them.' I had no problem on that score with an enforced £100 banger, but it was ironic that even my average customers could arrive in far superior cars to the so-called affluent landlord's.

My darts player, still in a state of shock and throwing spasmodic acid glares in my direction, began to dismantle his darts. 'Oh well, it'll be the Green Dragon for me in future,' he uttered with emotional tremor. 'They won't turn trade away.'

I lost a total of twelve customers to my neighbouring pub yet the increase in my turnover was a highly noticeable feature thanks to the more lucrative drinking tastes of my newly acquired clientele.

For some time I suffered the caustic tongues of a few casual darts types, but when I considered the Fox and Hounds, the most successful pub in the Vale, had no dartboard at that time, I felt that my action was not so heinous as my exiles would believe. As the year neared its end, on a bleak November morning I sped towards London on a comfortable South Wales Pullman with mixed feelings. The Bells was definitely going through a revival and I had been selected for interview in industrial sales. I had the sensation of racing for a goal that I didn't want to score as the train made its familiar rhythm through the gaunt English countryside. 'Tell them everything,' said my mind, 'hide nothing. You live in the Six Bells, and you're proud of it. Don't creep and crawl, you don't need the job really, the pub's coming back to life.'

Later that day as I retraced the down line to South Wales I knew I had been successful. 'We'd like all your loyalties, Mr Brock,' said the sales manager. 'With the best will in the world you would find it difficult to ignore the pub, so we would like you from there in, say, a year.' He ended in a combination of a request and a question which was mellowed with a forced smile. I agreed while playing for time. 'Damn it, I wasn't so sure I wanted to leave the cursed Bells' was my mind's answer as we hurtled into the hollow-sounding Severn Tunnel. The old nostalgic bug was burrowing into my very soul as I tried to visualise a life without the place. It was a family legend, Sylvia had been born there, her son had been born there, perhaps his child or Susan's child should be born there. I felt Bob Styles' feelings, a desire to covet the place for the family. 'Bloody masochist' said my unpredictable mind as the train lurched me back to reality over the rail crossings of Newport station. 'Your children would never tolerate the life-style for such a paltry reward. Get out while you're young and live your life with them.'

A week later I opened the envelope containing the result of my interview with shaking hands and a pounding heart.

'I've got it, Sylvia,' I said with a sigh and shrug of defeatism, which should have been an elated 'Whoopee'. 'I start a week Monday, London for a month's product knowledge training. How the devil are you going to manage?'

She hadn't heard my question, she was stunned, her freedom was just around the corner, and I don't think she wanted it. Like me she was a prisoner of the Bells, another reluctant, yet compulsive servant of Bacchus and John Barleycorn.

But we had the blessing of her father as we sat around the fire late that evening. 'To tell the truth,' he said with a sparkle in his mischievous eyes, 'we never made more than an average living here, but I liked the life. If it were not for the veg out of the garden and what I got with the gun we'd have starved half the time.' His heavy brogue shoe pushed an unburnt log end into the low fire to create a myriad of sparks against the black background of the chimney. 'Still,' he continued, 'it's no good flogging a dead horse. I honestly thought you two would have made a go of it, but the bloody breathalyser finished it.'

During the days leading up to my London departure the Bells intensified its hold on me, it caressed me, it hugged me, it talked to me and, for all my abuse of its ancient walls, I loved it.

13 · Time, Please

THE HUSTLE of London was in deep contrast to the placid Vale of Glamorgan, where the Six Bells played host in its own inimitable fashion as it had done for centuries. My father-in-law and Frank took turns to manage the house during my absence. Frank was a bricklayer by day who enjoyed his split-personality of barman by night. He was a very popular character who enlivened the pub greatly during those early sparse days of the breathalyser.

As the tube trains ferried me daily to my work in their noisy crowded claustrophobic way, I studied the faces of the metropolitan passengers with growing apprehension. Would I become one of these bored expressionless people? God forbid. By comparison the Bells was like a haven of rest despite the constant hard labour it demanded. Each morning as we rattled and lurched through the warrens of the capital I suppressed the compulsion to call it off and return to Penmark. My notice had not been tendered, the rumours of my leaving would eventually die the death and no one would be any the wiser of my intentions. But the month wore on in its tormenting fashion and soon I slept once more under the sagging horsehair and lathe ceiling of the ancient inn. The silence kept me awake after suffering thirty days of the London drone, and only the occasional cough of a cow and the hoot of an owl pierced the otherwise total void of sound as I fought for sleep with a confused mind.

The pub was holding its own to keep out of debt, and provide us with a very average living, without holidays and other luxuries, while my new job with its company car combined to present us with a new-found life of unaccustomed wealth. But we habitually stuck our heads into the sand over the prospect of leaving. Sylvia was showing signs of overwork as a result of my increased periods of absence, and while we could then afford to pay for help only Frank was available during the evenings. But suddenly, with the strange uneven pattern of life, our problems became minute when we learned through the village grapevine that Raymond had a terminal illness. The news shattered my silly illusion that our little country community was so pure and chaste that no ailment could possibly incubate in its wonderful natural environment so near to God.

I was subconsciously obsessed with a sense of immunity to all disease in the feeling that it thrived only in the over-populated urban hells of man's design, but this was all mind-play, and Raymond had received his sentence even in our secluded Vale. I felt sad when I served him nightly and his unusual voice droned on with its unique humour as he baited Shirty with an act that would merit any theatre.

I tried the usual optimistic theory within myself. The doctors may have got it wrong – they were not always infallible, damn it – there was no difference in him. But more sadness was yet to strike the small village when a 'floater' called at the pub some weeks later.

'Heard about Shirty,' he said in ghoulish excitement. 'Collapsed and died over at the Dragon.'

'When?' I answered, as my body took on stiff numbness.

'Just half an hour ago,' replied my informant. 'I was there, I saw it happen. Came in and ordered a pint he did, an' down he went, didn't touch a drop of it.'

I suppressed a compulsive smile over his last remarks, for Shirty himself would have made a great humorous issue of the affair in not taking the paid-for pint with him.

I think his funeral must have been a village record-breaker as far as attendance was concerned, and throughout the service I would picture his deep-lined and weatherbeaten face reminding me of the immense beer sales that he had created. No one seemed to know if he was telling one of his long stories prior to his massive heart-attack, or indeed if he anticipated it with his legendary phrase: 'That's the truth, if I was to be struck down now.'

Raymond, clearly in deep grief, managed to serve a lighter note as we conducted a drinking tribute to the Bells' most famous character. 'I always told the silly bugger he'd say it once too often,' he said as he stroked an eyelid with the knuckle of his index finger. Not many months later, true to the medical forecast, he also died, and the Bells was the poorer for their passing. Their early deaths stunned the regulars who, like myself, had visions of the two men haggling at each other with their witty cross-chat well into their eighties.

All too soon came our last Christmas at Penmark, for while we had not then presented our notice of termination, the action would be inevitable under the extreme pressure of our commitments. On that magic night near the end of 1968 we felt increasingly nostalgic before the old log fire in the fusty upstairs room where so many dreams were recalled. Even Susan with only ten years to her credit was starry-eyed with recollections of that creaking old inn.

The following day saw the annual pilgrimage of the hunt followers to Cowbridge Common, and to this day I am no more enlightened over the hypocrisy of the so-called animal kindness of the British. Not so the hunters, they are out for the kill, under a false premise of vermin control, but they admit to the outcome of their destructive bloody 'sport'. It is the vast general public who still mystify me in their blinkered attitude to animal kindness. Their dogs have become highly protected species to enjoy more devotion in some families than children, yet some of these same adults will attend a bullfight during a Spanish holiday. They rapture over the joys of spring as they spear the cooked rib of a new-born lamb at the dinner table and its toy poodle likeness with jewelled collar and painted nails waits for the bone. They ignore the atrocities of the vile calf trade as the veal entrée is ordered with a watering mouth from the menu. This is not a protest on my part, just a realisation of the great British lie, but the balance must be watched, for where does true animal welfare end? The anti-cruel sports people, for all their good intentions, may eventually wish to see anyone prosecuted for stepping on a woodlouse after they have abolished fox hunting. But I sold my beer to these people on that glorious Boxing Day and like a good landlord I kept my views to myself and the till rang its merry tune in my ears. As I near the end of this book, I have an awareness that keeping a country inn involves a good layman's knowledge of rural life on a par with, say, a City of London publican's insight to the Stock Exchange or Fleet Street. But there is always a first time as I discovered in the early months of 1969 when I called to collect Susan from a birthday party at a farm a few miles away.

A worried-looking farmer glanced across from a barn doorway as I pulled into his yard.

'Trouble?' I shouted.

'I'll say,' he answered with a shrug. 'Too much.' A large

Friesian cow was tethered to a bullring in the wall, while her distended belly convulsed in labour. A pair of calf hooves protruded from her rear end connected to a rope and block and tackle from the opposite wall.

'Wrong way round, and it won't budge any further,' said the farmer. 'I've phoned for the vet, been trying for hours to move the bugger, hardest one I've ever come across.' A large Citroën car came into the yard as I looked helplessly on the suffering mother. 'Bloody good vet is this bloke,' he continued with an air of optimism. 'Haven't been with 'em long, but he knows what he's up to, a farmer's vet he is, not one of them cat-and-dog blokes.'

The recipient of his praise sat on the car's tailgate, to pull on his rubber boots before entering the barn. He looked younger than thirty, a handsome man with a genial approach as he surveyed the cow. 'We'll have to turn it, Ted, you're not going to have much joy that way.'

The farmer nodded his approval as he began to unfasten the pulling tackle and the vet donned his green smock and covered his hands in antiseptic jelly. For fifteen minutes his arms worked inside the cow as deep as his elbows, and as dusk closed in fast his face shone with sweat in the red half-light of a winter evening.

'Switch on, Ted,' he shouted to the farmer, 'you can't be that bloody poor.'

'There's no light here to switch on,' answered Ted.

'That's just fine,' said the vet, withdrawing his arms in a gurgling suction. 'It'll have to be a caesarean and I jolly well can't do that in the dark, can I?'

Ted looked at me with frustration. 'Nearest powerpoint is in the milking parlour, and I haven't got an extension cable that'll reach that far.'

I knew I possessed quite a long lead over at the Bells. 'Tell you what,' I suggested. 'I'll take Susan home, and return with my lead, shouldn't take more than half an hour, will that do?'

The vet was loading his hypodermic syringe for a local

anaesthetic. 'It's Hobson's choice, isn't it?' he answered. 'But there shouldn't be much delay by the time I give her this and get ready for the op.'

Susan wanted to go back with me, but with visions of a rather gory sight I refused. I little realised at that tender age she would take up nursing to become a theatre sister. When I returned in complete darkness to illuminate the barn the cow was slowly sinking to the straw-covered floor. Her glazed eyes followed our movements as her laboured breathing created jets of vapour from her dilated nostrils on that chill winter's evening, and her huge belly vibrated with pain as she moaned low and pitifully in the agony of her difficult birth.

'Right,' said the vet to me, 'you hold the light, and let's have a look inside.' I suddenly became squeamish at the thought with the emphasis on my personal behaviour when the surgeon began to cut. My body tingled as my eyes became glued to his moving scalpel which seemed to travel endlessly along the cow's flank. Soon he arrived at the womb for his second cut to relieve a pressure of warm water, mostly into my rubber boot, as I knelt before the suffering beast. She looked back with maternal instinct as he felt her calf while shaking his head.

'It's dead, I'm afraid, Ted. A pity too, it's a fine bull calf.' He placed the black and white carcass near the mother's head and her large soft tongue began to lick it in futile contentment. I felt so sad for her and the farmer, but the calf was lucky – by virtue of its sex it would have enjoyed only a few weeks with its mother before suffering its ultimate agonising death for the cruel veal industry.

I pursed the two wounds for the vet to stitch and, three hours from the start of the drama, we washed ourselves in the kitchen of the farmhouse. I drove home with a great admiration for the vet and a feeling of self-satisfaction of an experience I would never have missed. But my life consistently runs in vivid peaks and troughs, as Susan confirmed when she met me at the car.

'We've got fox trouble again, Dad,' she said excitedly as I opened the door, 'I think there's four Marans missing.'

I followed her across the car park as she ran towards the chicken run with our powerful beam torch. There were feath ers in abundance, but no carcasses. Inside the henhouse jus eight Marans remained clucking nervously on their perch.

Susan grasped my hand. 'It must have been happening when you brought me back from the party. I heard the commotion ran in for the torch and came straight down here. The hen were in a terrible state, it was awfully creepy in the dark.'

Once again I blamed the sheer pressure of our varied dutie for the neglect of not locking them in for the night, and the incident helped to resolve any misgivings of our departure from the inn. It was nearly closing time when I joined Frank in the bar, where the conversation centred on an escaped pum from the local zoo. It had been sighted in various locations, and the obvious thought entered my mind that the Marans could have been its victims. It would have been a gem of a topic i Shirty and Raymond were alive, but the situation remained fairly tepid in their absence.

'They got quite a few hunting parties out after him,' said on informed customer. 'And there's a bloke from Cardiff with crossbow and tranquilliser dart, friend of the zoo people he is 'cause they don't want him shot like.'

By then I was fairly convinced that the puma had killed my chickens, for a fox would never take away four birds. Tha evening after closing time I carried the shotgun as I went abou my nightly routine of locking up, and I felt an increasing apprehension that the beam of my torch would suddenly con front a pair of large green eyes in the inky darkness of moonless night. Despite the loss of my hens I sensed the exhilaration of liberty the beast was enjoying after suffering years of confinement in its small prison cage, and I became more convinced of the false face of our animal welfare. consider the ultimate obscenity to be a caged bird and I long fo the day when humans will become sufficiently civilised to appreciate that birds were created to range free – and to *fly* Anyone can bring a wealth of bird life into their gardens as have done with various encouragements, and as I type these words I am aware of the beautiful songs of freedom from more than twenty different species near my house.

The reader might assume that I was more concerned with animal welfare than selling my beer, but just like my neighbours I had become absorbed in the country way of life, when every day provided interest. The puma was shot dead a few days later a mile or so from the Bells, and I was thankful that it, like the still-born calf, had left the control of man for possibly a better world.

House-hunting was taken seriously during March, but our needs were hard to meet. Most estate agents made a fruitless promise when we requested a rural situation within our very limited price bracket, but eventually we succeeded in purchasing a semi-detached in a country lane on the outskirts of Barry. It was near the end of May that I sat down one Sunday afternoon to write our notice of termination.

All the livestock had been sold with the exception of the remaining eight Marans, then nearly six years old. They made excellent broody hens while lacking in egg production, but my father-in-law couldn't resist their pheasant-rearing prowess, and they moved to his cottage to continue many successful years of motherhood. Soon, as the intimation of our leaving permeated through the area, and applications for the pub began to swamp the brewery, our trade increased with potential new tenants and inquisitive customers from neighbouring pubs. Bob Styles did quite well with offers for various wall adornments such as the muzzle-loading shotguns, the wall clocks and enough copper and brassware to fill an antique shop. The large stag's head over the fireplace that used to change its expression with the mood of the fire seemed to take on a supercilious look during an auction for its valued possession.

'I'll give you twenty quid each for those casks,' said a dealer from Cardiff, pointing to the row of six Victorian porcelain spirit barrels in beautiful glaze and goldleaf design.

Bob was wide-eyed as he spoke to me through the corner of his mouth. 'Twenty quid, bloody hell, I remember taking a lorry from the brewery years ago to collect 'em from all the pubs, too old-fashioned, they reckoned at that time. When we got back to the yard everyone started to use 'em as a coconut shy with lumps of coal from the boilerhouse nearby. Bloody hell, twenty quid. I can't believe it.'

It was agreed that nothing should be taken until our last night, for the pub would have completely lost its character with bare walls, but as the successful new tenant had not offered to purchase the fittings we had no option in selling to the eager buyers. The unexpected influx of wealth to Bob's pocket, however, had little soothing effect on his nagging obsession of slanderous landlords.

'I've heard dozens of the buggers when I was a drayman. I tell you, it's a bloody disease with 'em to run down their predecessor. You want to make sure that your engines, pipes and beer are perfect on takeover day, and draw a glass for the supervisor and the new bloke, ask 'em what they think of it.' His mischievous smile crossed his face. 'And when they say it's perfect, you turn to the supervisor and say "Now you heard that, so remind him of it when he starts moaning about me." '

But is it not a strange human trait within us all from prime ministers to shopkeepers to condemn our previous occupants regardless of the condition of the inheritance?

A wily old publican from Cardiff had a weak interest in the Bells. 'Thought it might be the sort of place to retire in,' he said from the counter one evening after introducing himself with a letter from the brewery.

'The perfect place,' I answered, 'if you can exist on the low income.'

He gave me a wink as he jerked his head in the direction of the cellar. 'You sell a drop of weekend water, do you?'

'Sorry?' I said, trying to construe his strange question.

'That's why you're not making bugger all,' he continued.

'There's precious little profit in a barrel of beer, you got to sell a bit of "Adam's Ale" with it.'

I smiled in naivety, for while the stories of watering were endless, no one really knows what a publican does in the secret confines of his cellar. To my father-in-law the action was utter taboo.

'A pub is judged on its beer,' he constantly warned me. 'You can play about with anything, even the lemonade, but never touch the ale.' He freely admitted that a brusque personality such as he had had to be soothed with the sale of perfect beer. 'It's those marmy, smarmy landlords you have to watch,' he would say. 'They got to behave like that when you're buying their expensive water.'

'I don't think you'd get away with that in this pub,' I said to the Cardiff licensee, but he was adamant in his belief.

'Nonsense,' he replied with a slight flare of temper. 'I've been doing it for years, had to, or there'd be nothing in the job.' He looked both ways along the bar before bowing his head towards me as he spoke in a lower voice. 'Eighteen to one I work on, and that's not killing the goose that lays the golden egg like.' He straightened up to blast his vein-tangled bulbous nose into the bright paisley handkerchief. 'You work it out, that's two gallons to the barrel, sounds a lot don't it, but in the pint glass it's less than a half inch of water. I've measured it many a time.'

I did some crude calculations to realise that even the Bells with its meagre four barrels a week could make a profit increase of nearly eight pounds, a third of a weekly wage in those days. But it was small wonder that I never saw the Cardiff publican again, who boasted of his twenty-barrel house, for the Bells to him would represent a picture of abject poverty with so little watering potential.

I consoled myself that our pending departure was perhaps fortunate after hearing such a startling revelation, for I doubt that my integrity could have remained untarnished with such a new-found temptation so near as the simple water tap. The length of our notice began to shorten rapidly toward our provisional date of October and soon we were well into our busiest month of August. The new tenants had been selected from a pub in the Rhondda Valley – a strange choice we thought, for there was absolutely no similarity in the two houses – as they were seeking semi-retirement from a very busy pub. I had my final brush with the hunt during August. They were cub hunting in the area, a free-for-all type of meet, where protocol and dressage is relaxed in pursuit of the young foxes. A party dismounted at the Bells and a particularly boisterous young male ordered their drinks. Now, it had long been the policy of country inns to serve draught beer in straight glasses or heavy tankards, subject to the customer's taste, and I politely asked the huntsman how he would like his served. He half turned from the counter to face his colleagues, of mixed sex, some in their pinks, others quite unconventional, as cub hunting permits.

'Look here, my man, I asked for a pint of beer. I'm not concerned how you serve it, so will you kindly get on with it before we all die of thirst.' He was rewarded with his antici-pated burst of laughter from an appreciative audience, but he had shattered all my pretensions of a good landlord and my wounded pride screamed within me for revenge. As I reached beneath the counter for any glass that came my way I was aware of the two-gallon stainless steel slop bucket on the floor near the beer engines. It was half full and destined to be thrown away, for sadly the pigs were no longer available for their tipple. I placed it on the counter before him, cursing myself for opening the pub on a day off only to become involved in a battle of honour. His smile vanished as he peered into the bucket.

'What the devil is that?'

'Well, you said you were not concerned how I served it,' I answered. 'But I reckon you'd look silly with just a pint, you're mouth needs something about this size.' I received a far greater ovation than my victim, who offered me his hand saying, 'You won that round, old boy, well done.'

I think I could have experienced no more suitable ending to my strained relationship with the hunting fraternity, and if the immortal words that refer to them as 'the unspeakable in full pursuit of the uneatable' are any criterion, then it is little surprise that I am so confused over these strange people.

As summer began to lose its warmth, we came to our final season at Penmark, the wonderful bronze spectacles of autumn. In a brief three months or less everything would be so skeletal and barren offering the cold hand of welcome to the northern blizzards. Or would there be rain instead to taunt the farmer, for the Vale is so unpredictable?

We suffered our usual nights of sea fog when the village, just two miles inland, listened to the mournful tone of the Nash Point horn, and the bar was void of careful motorists, who feared the combination of mist and breathalyser. But those were the nights of memories when only the villagers claimed the pub as their ancestors had done for centuries. Were these feelings just my own tender sentiments? Not really. My father-in-law always said, 'If I won the pools, I'd buy an isolated pub somewhere and run it just for myself and the villagers, but if profit was the true motivation a country pub is not the place to consider.'

Finally, and quite suddenly, there dawned our last working day at the inn, 18 October 1969, when everything would be moved to our new home, except our bed. The rooms began to sound with a cold unlived hollowness as the furniture and carpets were taken to the removal van for the short journey to Barry. I recalled how we had moved in from our little house around the corner, a washing machine one day, a chair another, over a period of several days and my father-in-law had done likewise, but this was so final, I thought. The Bells was going away from the family; how many times in the past had its old walls seen the same situation? We smiled at each other in the window of our bedroom as the remover's van pulled out of the car park. Behind us on the bare boards lay only the forlorn mattress made up in readiness for our final night, without the children, who were at the in-laws, and I tried to fathom Sylvia's mind as her eyes misted with nostalgia.

The afternoon was spent in preparing a cold buffet to be a farewell spread for our loyal customers, but by a strange coincidence that evening the pub began to fill rapidly, and by eight-thirty both bars were packed to capacity.

'We should have tried this every night,' I shouted to Sylvia above the bar noise as we fought to satisfy the demands of the sea of anxious faces before us. Most were recognisable as the casual floaters who had all concentrated at the Bells, for our farewell. We chose to accept their visit as a genuine mark of respect over our departure instead of a possible feeling of jubilation on their part.

Near ten o'clock, and as a complete surprise, came our presentation when a small deputation called for order and the normal loud conversation was reduced to a very unusual silence. A fine inscribed glass-domed clock was handed to Sylvia with quite an emotional farewell speech from their spokesman, and during his talk I believe we both felt a sense of modesty of not being as praiseworthy as his descriptions.

The evening was marred only by the absence of Shirty and Raymond, while my in-laws opted out in the face of a very sensitive experience for it was a total break for them after more than thirty years. I eventually rang the bell with a very carefree attitude to the clock, which had ruled my life, for nearly five years, and I could well envisage Bob Styles' forecast that for some considerable time I would habitually refer to it for opening and closing. 'The missus thought I was going potty when we first moved to the cottage,' he said. 'I actually went to open the front door a couple of times.'

And then it was over as the extractor worked at full speed to clear the smoke-laden air in the empty pub, which always seemed to sigh with relief after yet another night in its long history. If only you could talk, I often thought, as I looked around its ancient walls. We slept a restless sleep that night on our little mattress island on the sea of bare boards of that huge empty room; even our breathing sounded hollow as I waited for the dawn to work the cellar and beer systems into pristine condition for the newcomers.

While Sylvia cleaned the bars I pulled on the beer engines until my arms became like lead. I swear no beer pumps in the country could be cleaner after bucket upon bucket of soda and salt water had coursed through them, and finally I connected up to new casks just as Bob Styles arrived on the scene.

'Try that,' I said with a feeling of total exhaustion, as I drew him a half-pint of pale ale. He took a liberal draught after smelling the beer, and I received his accolade with deep pride when he drank the remainder. 'That's as good a pint as I ever served,' he said, smacking his lips. 'Wooden cask as well, you couldn't leave 'em a better pint.'

I was intrigued with his last remark. 'Don't tell me you can taste what cask it comes from?' It was the height of the transition period from wood to aluminium, and the mixture was so consistently even that I was not even aware of the type of cask from which he was drinking. He slapped a ten pence piece onto the counter with his usual wicked half-smile. 'I can taste the wood, two bob on it.'

I stepped into the cellar and my eyes followed the pipe line of pale ale to a wooden cask between two aluminium kils. Returning to the bar I placed my ten pence with his. 'Home Brew next,' I said, looking him straight in the eyes. 'Tell me what you think of it, and what type cask it's from.'

He repeated his tasting routine. 'Well, it's a nice one, but not from the wood, I'm afraid.'

He was right, but I was not convinced having been a victim of his practical jokes on so many occasions. 'You're either the world's profound expert on beer tasting or a bloody lucky guesser,' I said with a laugh, but on reflection I realise he really was a true connoisseur of ale, if there is such a title. At ten-thirty the inn was far more radiant than usual, purely for our short-lived ego, and the benefit of the new tenants who were supposed to believe that we always kept it that way. They arrived with their many helpers in a small convoy of two cars and a removal van to effect an instant occupation as we sat in the bar virtually unnoticed for I had relinquished my licence in court the previous day, and they were the new holders. With our mattress tied to the top of our car we waited for the brewery supervisor to complete his stock check of our goods and glasses when finally he brought us together around a table in the lounge. I accepted his word for the value of goods that the new tenant would pay and he handed me his cheque with a tired smile for he had already carried out the same final routine at his last pub.

I was suddenly aware of Ben the cat rubbing against my trousers; never an affectionate animal he seemed to be over-insistent in telling me that he also was ready to go and join Lady at our new home.

At precisely opening time we pulled out of the car park, not completely dry-eyed, with many memories of a saga ended: of the beer and its changeable moods; the customers whose palate is satisfied or offended; the animals, domestic and wild, who brought so much interest to our life; and the intoxicating atmosphere of the glorious Vale of Glamorgan. We had worked extremely hard to realise a total capital of £500, just enough to pay the deposit and legal fees of our new home, but it had been a worthwhile experience. My father-in-law called promptly the following morning to enlist my help. 'There's an old steel water tank at the rear of the Bells,' he said over a cup of tea. 'Just what I need at the top of my garden. I've phoned the new chap and he said it's all right for me to take it.'

I looked through the window where his car and trailer awaited us for yet another of his herculean tasks, for I was well aware of the proportions of the tank. Thirty minutes later we both recoiled in horror at the entrance to the pub's car park to see our beloved beer engines tossed into an ignominious heap near the cellar door. Their white porcelain handles with the willow patterns and ornate brass caps pointed forlornly in a rakish angle to the skyline like abandoned gun barrels on a battlefield. Their fine rosewood cabinets were engulfed in coils of pipeline that must have served countless thousands of pints.

Nearby stood the brewery maintenance van with its back doors open to reveal all the equipment for the installation of keg beer, the system whereby a top pressure of CO_2 gas forces sterile beer along a thin pipe to a gaudy little dispenser at the counter. It was the death of conventional draught beer at the Bells.

'All the cleaning for nothing,' I said with a laugh to Bob Styles. 'Does he realise that I got up at four-thirty in the morning to do them?'

But my father-in-law, in his inimitable fashion, attacked the new licensee vehemently as he appeared in the doorway. 'That's the end of good beer in that house, all wind and piddle from now on.' He lowered his tone to speak to me. 'If poor old Fred the ferret could see that lot he'd turn in his grave. Worked like a Trojan the day that we laid them into the lounge, remember?'

The new man responded with a smile. 'It's progress, Bob, you've got to keep abreast of the times.'

'Bullshit,' replied Bob, in another undertone for my ears. 'The public won't put up with that gassy rubbish for long. They'll demand the return to the real thing, I know 'em.'

At the time I thought he was displaying the older person's usual objection to change, but how right he proved to be when, in 1971, the Campaign for Real Ale was founded. The keg systems are being rejected as fast as they were originally installed in favour, in Wales and England, of old-style beer engines with decorative handpumps and, in Scotland, in favour of traditional air-pressure tall fonts. Some houses proudly serve their cask-conditioned ale with invitations prominently displayed outside to taste their traditional beers. The Six Bells is one such inn, and now Bob Styles can sleep peacefully beneath the sycamore trees in the church across the road.

TIME, LADIES AND GENTLEMEN, PLEASE